The Development of Handw

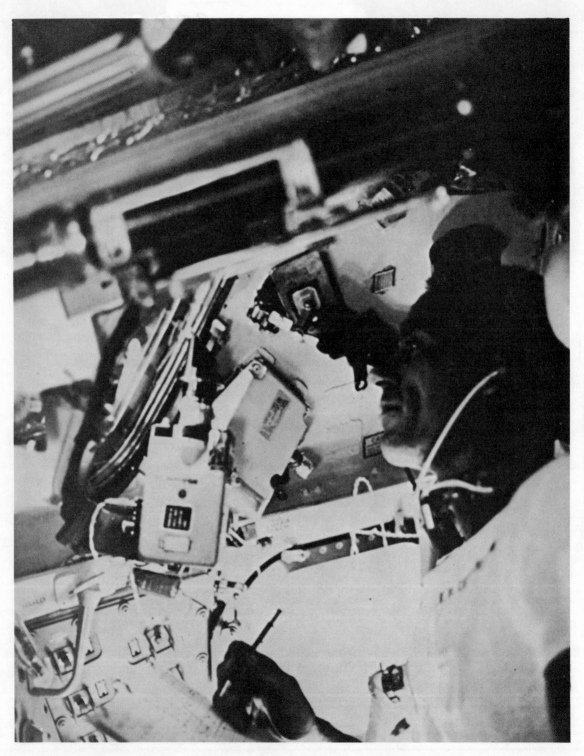

*Walt Cunningham writing inside the Apollo 7 spacecraft*

# The Development of Handwriting Skills

## A RESOURCE BOOK FOR TEACHERS

## CHRISTOPHER JARMAN M.Ed.

"The older virtues, as they are usually
called, of neatness, accuracy, care and
perseverance and the sheer knowledge
which is an essential of being educated . . .
are genuine virtues, and an education
which does not foster them is faulty."

*Plowden Report*, 1966: "Children and their
Primary Schools", para 506

BASIL BLACKWELL

ISBN 0631 19240 9 (Cased)
ISBN 0 631 19230 1 (Paper)

Printed and bound in Great Britain
by Billings & Sons Limited, Worcester.

# Contents

| | |
|---|---|
| *INTRODUCTION* | 1 |
| | |
| *BACKGROUND* | 2 |
| The Re-discovery of Traditional Handwriting | 2 |
| Handwriting in America | 4 |
| Handwriting in Australia | 6 |
| Handwriting and Personality | 8 |
| | |
| *DEVELOPMENT PROFILES* | 9 |
| Stages in Children's Handwriting | 9 |
| How to Encourage Handwriting Skills in Young Children | 16 |
| The Tools for Writing | 18 |
| The use of Lined or Unlined Paper | 19 |
| The Basic Patterns | 22 |
| Teaching the Patterns | 23 |
| ita | 30 |
| | |
| *A BASIC MODERN HAND* | 31 |
| Teaching the Letter Families | 33 |
| Three Rules for Good Handwriting | 41 |
| Children with Handwriting Difficulties | 42 |
| Awkward Pen-holds and Lefthanders | 43 |
| Reversal of Letters | 46 |
| | |
| *THE COPY PAGES* | 47 |
| Alphabet Sentences | 101 |
| | |
| *RESOURCES FOR PROJECT WORK* | 102 |
| Historical Development | 103 |
| The Development of Informal Handwriting | 109 |
| The Chancery Cursive or Italian Hand | 113 |
| The Rise of Copperplate | 116 |

| | |
|---|---|
| The Invention of the Steel Pen | 117 |
| The Invention of the Fountain Pen | 119 |
| | |
| *INTERESTING FACTS ABOUT WRITING* | 120 |
| | |
| Starting Points for Project Work | 121 |
| Useful contractions of words | 132 |
| | |
| *THINGS TO DO* | 133 |
| 1. Cutting a quill pen | 134 |
| 2. Weathergrams | 136 |
| 3. Flourishes | 138 |
| 4. Shaped writing | 139 |
| 5. Acronyms and Acrostics | 140 |
| 6. Decorated Borders | 142 |
| 7. Writing in Curves | 143 |
| 8. How to Write in a Spiral | 144 |
| 9. Decorated Capital Letters | 146 |
| | |
| *MATERIALS AND BOOKS* | 148 |
| Copybooks and cards | 148 |
| Books for Classroom Projects on Writing | 148 |
| Addresses for Equipment and Aids | 149 |
| American Suppliers | 149 |
| English Bibliography | 149 |
| Australian Bibliography | 149 |

# Acknowledgements

Any book on the development of handwriting skills is bound to be based upon the work of many other writers and scholars. I cannot therefore claim very much originality for the contents of this one. I am deeply indebted to my art lecturer at King Alfred's College, Winchester, Wilfred Hodgkinson, for his encouragement, and to all the authors, calligraphers and historians whose books I have devoured hour after hour since I was a schoolboy. It is impossible to list all the sources of one's information, but I should like to mention some of those whose personal help and advice I have been able to draw upon, either in conversations or correspondence. My grateful thanks are given to the following for their help in studying both the development of handwriting and the development of children.

William Aaron, Calligrapher
Phyllis Annis, University of Leicester
Leslie Bennett, Primary Adviser, Oxfordshire
John Coe, Senior Adviser, Oxfordshire
Barbara Getty, Teacher, Portland, Oregon, USA
Elizabeth Hitchfield, University of Warwick
Geoffrey Nockolds, Managing Director, Osmiroid Educational
Lloyd Reynolds, Reed College, Portland, Oregon, USA
Robin Tanner, HMI retd.
Villu Toots, Calligrapher, Estonia, USSR

Grateful thanks are also due to the following for permission to use written and pictorial material.

Anne Backhouse, Oxfordshire
Berkshire Education Authority
Bodleian Library, Oxford
Kunsthistorisches Museum, Vienna
Dr. A. E. Osley of the Society for Italic Handwriting
Osmiroid Educational, Gosport
Oxford University Press
Society of Scribes and Illuminators
Unwin Bros. Ltd.
Joyce Whalley, Victoria and Albert Museum
Finally, thanks to my wife Sally for her patient typing.

# Introduction

When Marshall McLuhan published 'The Gutenberg Galaxy' in 1962, many people began to assume that the age of handwriting was over. Indeed, some believed that McLuhan's genius foresaw the disappearance of the printed word altogether. After fifteen years these assumptions already seem curiously dated. The publishing of paperback books has mushroomed alongside the growth of television; and the public demand for skills in the three R's has become a major political issue in most western countries, as well as in the newly developing nations. It seems that nothing electronic is likely to take the place of the quick handwritten note on a piece of paper. Mr. McLuhan himself should be given credit for understanding this. His writings were intended as warnings to help us to realise the dangers, as well as the benefits of modern media. He understood the values of permanency, and the importance of reflective thinking implicit in communicating through printed or handwritten words. McLuhan wrote, 'Far from wishing to belittle the Gutenberg mechanical culture; it seems to me that we must now work very hard to retain its achieved values'.

Hence this book is an attempt to bring together some of our twentieth century understanding of child development with the 'achieved values' of a cultural heritage. Our pupils will continue to need to write by hand for many years to come. Both they and their teachers, therefore, should know something of how the alphabet and our handwriting came about, and of how they may learn its skills at the appropriate stages.

In the Department of Education and Science Report 'A Language for Life' published in 1975, in the section on handwriting, the following important points are made:-
The ability to write easily, quickly and legibly affects the quality of a child's written output, for difficulty with handwriting can hamper his thoughts and limit his fluency. If a child is left to develop his handwriting *without instruction* he is unlikely to develop a running hand which is simultaneously legible, fast flowing and individual and becomes effortless to produce. We therefore believe that the teacher should devote time to teaching it and to giving the children ample practice. . . . Children should grow up accustomed to taking care in the way they present their work and to regarding its appearance as an important aspect of the whole production.

The methods and hints shown in this book on how to teach children are not 'theoretical'; nor have they been developed to suit a static population from just one particular school. I have been very fortunate to have taught and learnt from thousands of children and hundreds of teachers from all parts of the country. Having taught in many schools, colleges and teachers' centres, I find that ideas which are unacceptable or do not work are thrown out or refined by the students themselves.

The teacher who studies the various sections carefully should gain enough confidence to develop her own practice and to teach a basic modern hand to any age of pupil.

This book has been written with the future in view, bearing in mind that we cannot re-invent the alphabet which has served us so well for over 2,500 years!

1

# Background

## The Re-discovery of Traditional Handwriting

Between 1870 and 1876 William Morris, the Victorian designer and author, practised writing the old medieval style. The original art and skills of writing and lettering had become lost. Even well-known artists and printers of Victorian times did not know how the early manuscripts were prepared or written. The use of the broad-nibbed quill was almost unknown. When William Morris died in 1896 he had stimulated an interest in the revival of early Arts and Crafts which is still going on today in Europe and America.

In 1897 Edward Johnston, a young medical student, gave up his studies to investigate the old manuscripts and penmanship in the British Museum. Gradually, most of what we now know about the use of quills, inks, the preparation of vellum and the design of our alphabet was re-discovered by Johnston in his researches. The details of his work were published in his book 'Writing, Illuminating and Lettering' in 1906.

*Print Script Introduced*

In 1913 Edward Johnston suggested, in a lecture to London teachers, that a simplified skeletal form of the Roman alphabet, which he had studied in the twelfth century Winchester Bible, might be a good model for young children.

By 1916 many London schools and others in America and Australia were teaching this 'print script', as it appeared to be so much more sensible and legible for five and six year olds than the 'copperplate' (see p. 116) attempted with the pointed steel nib. Her Majesty's Inspectors of Schools had long asked for an improved system for beginners in school, and print script seemed ideal.

Unfortunately, none of the infant teachers at that time were also trained calligraphers. And, while the appearance of print script was excellent, the hand movements used in its construction were not. Many teachers and children were taught to perceive the letters as a 'ball and stick' framework. This encouraged a system of building up letters from separate parts, which is exactly the opposite training to that needed for a flowing handwriting. Nicolette Gray, in a cogent article in *The Times Educational Supplement* 19.8.77, put the argument against print script very well.

a b c d e f g
h i j k l m n
o p q r s t
u v w x y z

By the mid 1930s a serious obstacle to children's handwriting development had arisen in both England and America. At some time in every child's school life he was required to change over from print script to 'joined' writing, or 'double' writing as it was often called. This was a complete denial of the important teaching principle 'Start as you intend to go on'.

A London County Council District Art Inspector attempted quite successfully to improve matters. This was Marion Richardson who, in 1935, produced her famous copy-books in a joined style, half way between italic and copperplate, and using a broad nib. Her joined, cursive style was recommended for infants right from the start. When taught well, this is a very legible hand.

> The race took so long, the riders having to go round the course so many times, that people went on complacently with their tea, only looking out occasionally to see how things progressed, watching the riders go by – one with bright red braces, one in a blue cotton coat, two middleaged men in their best bowlers and one, obviously too well mounted for the rest, in correct riding dress. They came round each time in the same order – the correct one, red braces, blue coat and the bowlers last. Evidently the foremost one knew he could easily win, and the others had decided that 'it was to be'. In the machine like regularity of their advent, their unaltered positions and leisured pace, they were like hobby horses.
>
> From Gone to Earth by Mary Webb.

*Writing by a mature pupil aged 17 who had been taught by Marion Richardson's methods since the age of 11. An example taken from the teacher's book to 'Writing and Writing Patterns' (Hodder and Stoughton).*

3

In 1932, three years earlier than Marion Richardson, Alfred Fairbank had published his book 'A Handwriting Manual'. Only a small number of schools became interested in this revived Italic hand, possibly because the instructions were not aimed directly at the youngest schoolchildren.

In 1957 Fairbank co-operated with Charlotte Stone of the Froebel Institute in London to produce the very fine set of school copybooks known as 'Beacon Writing', published by Ginn & Co. A rush of italic copybooks were published in the 1950s and an upsurge of interest in this traditional hand took place in many British primary schools. In 1952 the Society for Italic Handwriting was formed. An excellent quarterly journal is published by the society. Enquiries should be made to the Secretary, S.I.H.,

Mrs. Fiona Sturdy,
69, Arlington Road,
London N.W.1.

or to the American Secretary

Mrs. Jo Anne DiSciullo
6800 S.E. 32 Avenue, Portland,
Oregon 97202, USA.

Various copybooks, cards and wallcharts are now available, all of which owe a great deal to Alfred Fairbank's energy in reviving the basic Italian hand for modern use. A full list of recommended books and aids is given at the end of this book.

## Handwriting in America

In 1791 John Jenkins of Boston published the first American manual of handwriting. The style was known as 'Round Hand' but was the early commercial copperplate based upon italic and given the engraver's fine loops. There were three editions of this popular book, the last in 1816.

By about 1825 steel pens began to be used in America, replacing the turkey quill. They sold for about forty cents apiece at first, but became cheaper as they became more common.

Other well-known writing masters were Benjamin Franklin Foster of Boston, and Henry Dean of New York. Like most American masters, both called themselves Professors of Penmanship.

In 1848 Platt Rogers Spencer published his system which became widely known in the USA and used throughout the nineteenth century. This system was highly embellished, particularly the capital letters. The writing was done in fine lines with a steep slope and occasional thick downstrokes on descenders and capitals. Spencerian writing really set the pattern for the modern American hand.

By 1900 Charles Paxton Zaner in Columbus, Ohio and Austin Palmer in New York were running successful publishing companies selling their own style of copybooks. In the interests of speed, the thick and thin shading of Spencerian was eliminated, and the uniform lines of the American business hand began. It has been taught almost universally ever since. To a European eye Americans all appear to write in a very similar style. This goes to prove the point, however, that we only notice individuality in styles with which we are most familiar. The illustration shows most clearly how the 'manuscript' and the cursive do not share the same hand movements.

*Seeing America is like seeing the world. We have many kinds of farms and industries. Our people do many kinds of work.*

## Seeing America is like seeing the world. We have many kinds of farms and industries. Our people do many kinds of work.

*From* Guiding Growth in Handwriting *by Frank N. Freeman Ph.D. Published by the Zaner-Bloser Co., Columbus, Ohio, 1970 Edn.*

In recent years, under the influence of a genuine Professor of Art, Lloyd Reynolds, lately of Reed College, Portland, Oregon, the Italian hand has been re-introduced into many Oregon schools. Research by Dr. Charles Lehman has produced a very fine scheme of simple writing from kindergarten onwards, which it is hoped will be an improvement upon the print script – business hand gap, which still bedevils the American Grade School system.

5

## Handwriting in Australia

The major influence on handwriting styles in Australia was the emphasis on calligraphy and 'a clear, neat hand' that came from Victorian Britain and, in particular, Scotland. Until the 1930's the letter forms practised in schools were based on those found in the copy books of the late nineteenth century. This 'copperplate' style was common to all Australian states, with minor variations, until the late 1950's, when several State Education Departments developed scripts based on Marion Richardson's 'joined style'.

Similar, too, was the approach to penmanship. Not only were improving maxims ('Waste not, want not') the basis of copybook (or blackboard) practice, but the slope and the shape of the letters were built on the repetition of structured exercises. There was considerable stress on correct posture and meticulous copying.

Post-Federation saw the development of distinctive, and prescriptive, styles in each state and, although the standardised forms of earlier times have given way to the provision of *suggested* styles and guidelines, this variation remains today.

Each of the six State Education Departments has a preferred style. In most, individuality and the teaching of different styles is encouraged.

The objectives of teaching handwriting set by the Victorian Education Department would be shared by all:

To recognise handwriting as a skill that must be developed.

To develop both a legible style and fluency in handwriting.

To develop and maintain the printing skills.

To develop positive standards of neatness and pride in handwriting.

*Simon and Andrew tune into Australia's School of the Air from their home on an isolated sheep station in Western Australia.*

6

These examples from a current handbook for Australian teachers demonstrate the difficulty of schools faced with a tradition of 1913 print script for infants. The choice of 'Modified Cursive' or a kind of 'Square Gothic' is then given to the third grade. This last style departs too far from the traditional oval shape to be recommended as an everyday hand.

*Infants*

# a quick brown fox jumps over the lazy dog.

*Third Grade*

*A quick brown fox jumps over the lazy dog.*

*Third Grade*

# "What wisdom can you find that is greater than kindness?" – Rousseau.

# Handwriting and Personality

There is a widespread belief that handwriting reveals your personality or your character. Respectable psychologists have been prepared to admit the truth of this for the last thirty years, and although a number of small studies of graphology have been made, it is still a promising area for further research.

A famous psychologist, Gordon Allport of Harvard University, has stated quite categorically that 'graphologists' are able to diagnose some characteristics from a person's handwriting to a degree beyond those arrived at by chance. There is, says Allport, a strong case to be made for handwriting analysis because it can be described as 'crystallised gesture'. Psychologists have invented instruments for measuring the three dimensions of handwriting, its pressure, width and vertical length.

In the 1920s a German psychologist called Klages maintained that handwriting was a good example of the conflict of man's two layers of personality, the 'coping' part and the 'expressive' part. In coping, the learner is adapting himself to the copybook conventions in order to write. He must conform to the cultural expectations. On the other hand his expressive layer needs to rebel against the school copy in his own individual way. He shows his energy, aggressiveness, hostility, fear, ambition or rigidity in the ways in which his handwriting departs from the standard copy. The skilled graphologist is able to interpret some of these departures.

Handwriting is culturally imposed. A Japanese or a Russian child will learn quite different shapes in order to convey on paper the same thoughts as a British or Australian pupil and since personality in a human being is something which grows and develops within a cultural context, it would be a mistake to expect to read too much from immature handwriting. During the learning process it must be accepted that children's writing will be *fairly characterless*. Sometimes a particular teacher may impose a marked personal style upon a whole class, but this should not be confused with the character development of the child himself. Allport writes that a six year old will laboriously copy letters or numbers as precisely as he can from his copybook or from his teacher's blackboard model. His graphic production has virtually no individuality. The written papers on the classroom display board are almost all alike. With regard to handwriting young children are prisoners of their culture. Towards puberty true individuality in handwriting begins to appear. By then the child has mastered the cultural forms; they are second nature to him. He begins to take liberties with them. His formation of letters, slant, embellishments, are his own. All this experimenting need not be conscious, but it clearly violates the original cultural model. Finally, the graphic style settles down, adapted to the individuality of the person. Handwriting is simply one example of the compromise we all reach between cultural obedience and individual integrity.

# Developmental Profiles

## Stages in Children's Handwriting

In order to avoid undue pressure on children, the teacher should be completely familiar with the standard of handwriting one should expect from children at different ages and stages. While it must be re-emphasised that children's perceptions and motor development grow at differing rates, a rough guide is given here.

It is quite possible to obtain extremely precocious standards of handwriting with young children. Excellent copperplate has been achieved by whole classes of six year olds and beautiful adult calligraphy *can* be done by pupils of seven or eight. In such cases, however, I have invariably found that far too many hours of practice have been devoted to the mere skill, and other important aspects of children's education have been neglected in the process. It is possible for any teacher to become over-enthusiastic about one aspect of the primary school curriculum to the detriment of the children's overall development. It must be remembered too that young children are trapped in the classroom both by convention and the law. They will tolerate a great deal, knowing no other class with which to compare their lot. Later, when they grow older, they may well discard a skill which has been too forcefully or too prematurely imposed.

More than thirty years ago Arnold Gesell of the Yale Clinic of Child Development studied the writing behaviour of over sixty children as they grew up from five to ten years of age.

The following profiles, while owing much to Gesell's study, are based on more up-to-date observations, and should give teachers an idea of the levels of skill to be expected at different ages.

As with all brief descriptions of stages, they must not be too closely related to the age and ability of any particular child. But for those who have not had the opportunity to study the efforts of many children learning to write, this table may help to make their expectations more realistic.

### From 3 to 5 years old

At three years, children like to play at writing letters to people. They will often want to put them in envelopes and stamp them too. Children will begin to make lines of scribble across a sheet of paper.

By the age of four, children will be printing some letters of the alphabet, especially their own initials or the initials of words important to them, e.g. A for Alan, M for Mummy. Children may begin writing words very large

9

on scraps of paper and on drawing books. They like to copy single letters and familiar words but will not as a rule spend very long on these activities.

It has been common practice for adults to give children of pre-school age capital letters to copy, but they will copy small letters equally happily if given the examples.

At five they are usually ready to copy printed words and sentences, but find difficulty in understanding adult joined handwriting. Some five year olds who are early readers can begin to write and read a joined cursive style, but this is fairly uncommon.

Most five year olds will copy words printed for them in large irregular letters. If guidelines are used, little notice will be taken of them, and capital letters and small letters are often mixed indiscriminately. Some five year olds begin to reverse letters even if they did not do so at four. At this stage children often leave out a letter in a word, or a number in a row of digits.

*Five year old writing*

a witch. the spanish lady did not like the witch in her garden because she made spells to make her flowers and rose bushes disapear. the spanish lady put an alarm clock in the garden. the witch came the witch heard the alarm she ran out of the garden and never came back again.

Writing at this age is often seen as a rather boring task. Boys especially find it tiresome to write more than two or three lines. A great deal of encouragement is needed from adults. The early novelty of writing like a grown-up has probably worn off. Large differences in ability begin to show up, and while one or two very competent readers and writers may shoot ahead, it is unfair to expect the majority of children to write as much as the few.

At six, it is normal for children's letters to vary greatly in size. These will often get larger across the page from left to right. Children will write two or three lines at the top of a page and leave the rest blank. They will often write an undulating line of words or a line that droops down towards the end or swoops upwards!

There will still be consistent reversals of some letters and numbers, especially b, d, s, and 2, 3 and 7. Some capital letters which are important to them will remain in the middle of words. Often their own initial, such as B for Brian, will stay as a capital e.g.

*aBout*

I am a ball of clay the man is
stretching me. His warm hand is putting
more water on me he's pressing
and pulling me into shape. Now I am
a cider jar. I can feel the farmers
wife putting cider in me. Now she
is carrying me out to the field the
cold cider is splashing about inside
me. I lay down for a long time. I feel
the hot sun. A rough hand picks
me up and pours cider out of me

11

A few children are now able to write quite well. They begin to differentiate between the shapes of capital letters and small letters, although often not between their relative sizes.

In some cases, the more able children will begin to join letters and write a simple cursive hand. Many of the hitherto reluctant six year olds now want to write stories or to record their experiences in writing. Seven year olds become very anxious about spelling and are constantly erasing words and asking for their correct spellings.

Sevens can get quite fussy about their writing implements, expressing a strong preference for this or that type of pencil. A proportion of children, particularly girls, are ready for pen and ink in their seventh year, although many schools are surprisingly reluctant to encourage their use. This is a good time to introduce the more competent left-handed writers to a specially designed left-handed pen nib. By this age children are beginning to like ruled lines or an underlay for writing on. Writing may suddenly change size overnight. Some sevens begin to write very small indeed.

At this stage the teacher should spend some time reminding children about a relaxed pen hold and a good writing posture. Sevens will write in any corner of the room and in the most awkward body positions.

One day long ago there was a water pump and the people used to pump the water out of the water pump every morning to have a wash. One morning a little boy went to the water pump to get some water there was a big icicle hanging from the spout the boy put his hand on the handle and it was frozen stiff

There will be great individual differences now among the children of varying ability. At this age neatness in handwriting does not necessarily correlate with intelligence. Some girls, who are otherwise quite slow learners, may begin to copy and write very neatly. On the other hand highly intelligent and articulate children may have the most careless and untidy scrawls. It is at this stage that really concrete help from the teacher is needed. Admonition is useless, but the presentation of good examples to trace or copy, and the careful teaching of basic rules for letter shapes will help enormously.

Eight year olds sometimes begin to space their words very wide apart, resulting in only three or four words to a line.

By this age most children write their numbers correctly but there may still be the occasional reversed letter such as d, b and s. At this stage too, p and g may still stand on their tails on the line. By now most children should be joining the letters where appropriate.

To me the Octopus has eyes that shine like gold.
With eight fat wriggley leggs that wrap round
you, and hold you firmley.
Down his legs are suckers.
His suckers could blind anyone who went near him
with out there eyes covered. If a man wanted to kill an
octopus he haust have a partner one for the bait and
one for the killer.
The man that is the bait must go and let the octopus
see him so the killer can kill much easier.
The octopus lives in a cave that is dark and spooky
the walls have faces like monsters that were shaped
with a knife many years ago.

Children from nine onwards now begin to develop a personal running hand if taught well. They normally feel a need to express themselves in writing, and to record stories. At this age they particularly like to write, bind and cover their own books on topics of personal interest. Three or four children in a class may develop a really keen interest in fine calligraphy and may practise handwriting and lettering for hours. For most children, however, handwriting becomes a utility, a means whereby other work may be done. Some will write for long periods without being bored.

From nine to eleven years, children's writing still retains an immature quality and the writing of the members of one particular class or grade level will look very similar, at least to the casual eye. By this age only children with emotional problems, severe motor control problems or other specific handicaps are likely to have really poor handwriting. Some parents, nevertheless, will expect too much from ten to eleven year olds, thinking that they should write as fast and as fluently as an adult. Pressure from this kind of over-expectation can cause severe setbacks in a child's handwriting development. It is not until between fourteen and fifteen years of age that anything approaching the person's mature adult hand develops.

*nine year olds writing*

Usally Mum does not let me go out in the rain but I was coming home from building a camp and so it was O.K.. On the 2nd of September there was a great big puddle and we splashed in it all the time. When we got splased the water felt wet and cold. Up at hill rise there is a huge puddle 9 cms deep and when you go though it you make water splash 4 ft in the air.

Where.

Monkeys in a forest
Beggerman in rags,
Marrow in a knucklebone
Gold in leather bags;

Dumplings in the oven,
Fishes in a pool,
Flowers in a parlour,
Dunces in a school;

Feathers in a pillow,
Cattle in a shed,
Honey in a beehive
   And babs in a bed.

## How to Encourage Handwriting Skills in Young Children

The various physical skills and mental abilities of children develop in a complicated arrangement which is unique to each individual. We do know, however, that there are standard sequences of development in all human beings which cannot be changed. That is to say, we all crawl before walking and walk before running. In the fields of perception and cognition there are similar invariable sequences. In these sequences children's understanding proceeds from the sensory-motor stage of groping, feeling and exploring by touch and movement, through simple comparing, matching and imitation, to independent abstract thought. It is known, nevertheless, that individuals pass through these stages at very different rates. The difference in pace is brought about by a combination of inherited traits, particularly physical abilities, and the kind of stimulation and experiences received in early childhood.

The skills of handwriting are of course only a relatively minor part of a child's overall development and education. It is helpful to teachers and parents to study the development of the acquisition of handwriting so that teaching may be given which will match the stage and needs of a child, rather than run counter to them.

First, it must be emphasised that handwriting is primarily a physical process. All handwriting experiences or lessons must be viewed as physical activities. A handwriting lesson is a 'movement' lesson in miniature. This means that a child's level of motor development is an important gauge against which to measure his handwriting needs. In particular, of course, it is the fine motor development which demands exercising. The following activities are well suited to encouraging early handwriting skills with pre-school children, infants, or those children who are retarded in these skills at any age:

Sorting little toys and bricks etc. into boxes.
'Posting' shapes into shaped holes.
Clay and plasticine modelling.
Cutting with scissors, especially cutting along lines.
Pasting cut-out shapes.
Jigsaw puzzles.
Tracing line drawings.
Following mazes with pencil or fibre-tip.
All forms of free drawing.
Dot-to-dot pictures.
Colouring in pictures with crayons or fibre-tips.
The tracing or copying of certain patterns.
Collecting cut-out letters.
(N.B. Not all pattern work promotes good handwriting skills. Some patterns lead to poor perceptions, and undesirable hand movements. These are discussed later.)

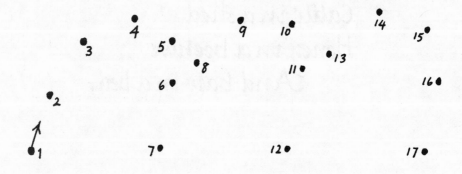

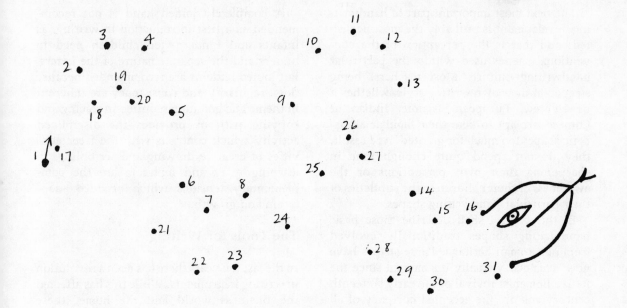

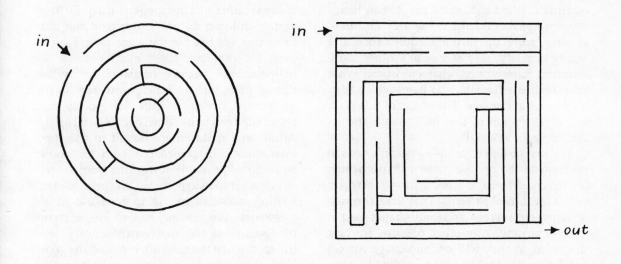

The next most important part of handwriting development is probably the most neglected; and that is the perception of the conventional shapes used within the particular handwriting culture. Most teachers, being steeped in their own writing style, whether it be Hebrew, European, Islamic, Indian or Chinese, are apt to take their familiar alphabetic shapes too much for granted. As a result, they do not spend quite enough time in sharpening their own perceptions or the awareness of their children to the subtleties of their particular handwriting shapes.

In this book I shall describe those basic handwriting shapes traditionally evolved from our Roman heritage. These shapes have now remained virtually unchanged since the Italian humanist revival of the early sixteenth century and are the accepted currency of all modern European and American writing. They are slowly coming into use in China and Japan, and Russian handwriting also consists of most of the same basic forms. (See page 131)

The various minor differences in so-called styles such as the Civil Service, Spencerian, Marion Richardson etc. should be seen as non-essentials. What is *basic* to the Roman handwritten alphabet is *basic* to them all. Children, as they grow up through adolescence and young maturity, may choose to acquire many different handwriting characteristics. What they need is a fundamental hand which they may use as a base line. The object of this book is the perception of this basic hand, and its development as a skill.

The first task in developing perception is to understand the precise pattern shapes which are involved in basic handwriting. There are only a few useful patterns. They arise through selecting certain regular, family shapes used in cursive writing. Any other patterns are best discarded, as they will not encourage correct hand movements. The idea prevalent in some schools that almost any pattern work is good handwriting practice is a mistaken one, and probably responsible for a good deal of poor shape perception.

A completely joined hand is not recommended as a first introduction to writing, as infants and kindergarten children need to understand the separate nature of the letters. But joined *patterns* are recommended because flow, regularity and consistency are inherent in them. The imitation required in tracing and copying patterns provides the disciplined activity which contrasts with the freer activities of creative drawing and scribbling. In learning, play and imitation are the complementary tensions which produce adaptation and growth.

## The Tools for Writing

In the last ten years there has been a revolution in writing instruments. While this has affected the business world and the home, these changes have not generally been reflected in the writing tools used in classrooms. Three quarters of eleven year olds still do all their work in pencil, while most twelve to fifteen year olds use ballpoints. Whereas at one time it was considered a purist plea that all children should use a fountain pen, such an attitude today is rather like insisting upon a quill. Most young children do not understand the term fountain pen, but use the name cartridge pen even for the lever-filled models. Even the ballpoint has become outdated by nylon-tipped pens, plastic rollerpoints and so on. Very hard fibre-tips with fine points or a chisel edge can be obtained cheaply and easily. Adults and children are bound to use these instruments. In accordance with the sound educational principle of working from the real environment, I suggest that all these modern writing tools can be put to good use in the classroom. We are inclined to laugh at the pedagogues of the nineteenth century who frowned when the steel nib replaced the goose quill. If we now cling to the metal nib, are we not being a little like them? Early objections to the ballpoint were largely due to the uneven ink line which it laid down. This is no longer true. The hard fibre-tip can be a beautiful writing instrument with the 'feel' of a well-cut reed pen about it. It should surely be our aim for children to write well and legibly and at a good speed with *any instrument*. For some children the special joy of fine calligraphy with a broad italic nib could be their main achievement. For others, to write swiftly and well with a pencil or a ballpoint may be sufficient. As teachers, we should be flexible enough to retain the motivation of any child when a particular writing instrument is important to him. We should certainly make ourselves masters of all writing tools as part of our own professional skills. The basic movements, basic patterns, basic shapes and basic joins can be done well with any instrument. The secret is a simple one. Teacher, teach yourself first!

Much of the quite unjustified criticism of italic handwriting has come, not because of the style, but because of the poor teaching of it by those who concentrated upon the 'special' nib and 'thicks and thins' with no understanding of the fundamental letter shapes. This has resulted in many schools teaching a barbaric, spiky and illegible gothic script and labelling it italic. This is unfair to a fine traditional and legible style.

## The Use of Lined or Unlined Paper

Teachers seem to argue quite fiercely about whether children should use lined paper to write on. At one time I thought that the argument was only 40 or 50 years old. Now that I have discovered that it goes back at least four hundred years, I have become less concerned one way or the other.

Some modern authorities recommend plain paper for the *youngest* children to practise on. This is a good idea. Little children can only concentrate upon one aim at a time, and we would wish them to be concentrating on forming the letters with the correct hand movements initially.

There is no doubt that for children above the age of about seven years, their writing looks much neater if done either on feint guidelines or using an underlay set of lines beneath plain paper. After all, most adults like to use this simple ruse with their notepaper.

A few years ago lined paper in school books used to be printed with lines very close together (5 or 6 mm). The space left between was too narrow and cramping for the five to seven year olds to develop rhythmic movements. In my experience, it is not *whether* lines are used or not that matters, it is *how* they are used. Lines which are spaced closer than 8 mm prove very inhibiting to children under eleven years, whether feint printed or from an underlay. For children under seven years I would provide lines at least 15 mm apart.

It is not the line upon which the writing *rests* which causes problems in handwriting development. It is the line above the writing. This can provide either a ceiling to depress the correct height of ascenders or, worse still, a tempting high line of achievement, drawing capital letters and ascenders up thoughtlessly to its height merely because it is there.

The teacher should guard against the temptation of using the line above as a measure or gauge for the height of ascenders. This can result in very unbalanced proportions of capital letters to small letters as well as to ascenders.

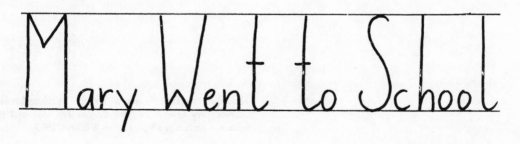

I have seen plenty of examples of this exaggerated use of the upper line. It is a great hindrance both to speed and legibility!

A base line upon which to rest the writing *is* useful and a valuable aid to page layout and neatness. Any further lines or sets of lines, e.g. marking the heights of minims and lengths of descenders etc., tend to promote short-term mechanical neatness which is lost when these 'crutches' are taken away.

Perhaps that most accomplished sixteenth century writing master, Peter Bales, could be our guide. He wrote in 'The Writing Schoolemaster' in 1590

Make ruled lines, the way more plaine to showe;
For children first must creep before they goe.
Although some simple sort absurdly say,
That writing first by rule is no good way:
Nay this I finde as triall due assignes,
Tis good at first, to write between two lines.

In medieval times and in Bales' day, writing was generally placed (by adult writers) 'between two lines' in this way.

*And alwaies beware, you will not write too fast*

*For writing fast, before you write the better,*

*Will cause at last, you make not one good letter.*

I would not suggest that children write in this way today. However, many will spontaneously do so.

An interesting piece of research in some British Primary Schools in 1974 showed that children of 6 to 7 years of age improved their legibility of writing, and their 'overall structure of work' when lined paper was provided.

The teachers, who had previously provided unlined paper, were so impressed with the children's improved work that they changed their policy.[1] Lines 20 mm apart and 10 mm apart were used in the experiment with equal success. On the opposite page an underlay of 15 mm lines has been printed.

[1]Burnhill, Hartley, Fraser & Young. 'Writing Lines an Exploratory Study' in *Programmed Learning and Educational Technology* Vol. 12 No. 2 March 1975.

## The Basic Patterns

The basic patterns for handwriting development are:-

1. mmmmmmmmmmmmm

2. ccccccccccccccc

3. uuuuuuuuuuuuuu

4. wwwwwwwwwwww

5. ururururururururu

6. mmmmmmmmmmm

7. oooooooooooooo

8. ililililililililililili

These are not in a strict order, and teachers
will have different views about which patterns to introduce first. Some children may
spontaneously begin with any pattern similar
to one of these eight forms. In which case, it
might be wise to start with that precise hand
movement with that particular child. But
eventually each child should be able to
reproduce all these patterns fairly exactly.
They should be especially helped to understand the subtle oval shapes, and the pro-
portions of the ascenders and descenders in
relation to the body of each pattern.

## Teaching the Patterns

These are suitable for very young children as soon as they are able to hold a pencil, say from 3 to 5 years, and for remedial work in handwriting with older children and adults.

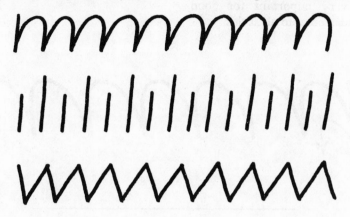

They will result in all kinds of attempts e.g.

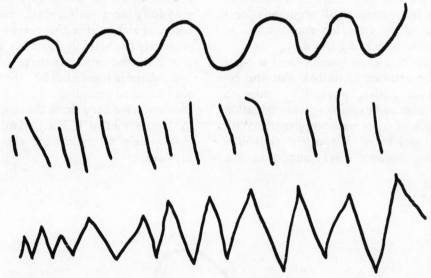

Do not be discouraged. A child has a lot to learn at this stage, namely
1. Perception of the pattern;
2. Which end of the pencil to write with;
3. Hand and arm muscle control;
4. How to grip the pencil;
5. How to stop the paper from moving;
6. Copying skills, such as transferring his attention from the pattern to his own paper and remembering it;
7. Left to right movement of a writing pattern;
8. Matching for size and height of pattern and many other new skills such as sitting still, listening to an adult's instructions and so on.

To begin with, use plain paper and any pencil, fibre-tip or crayon which is comfortable for the child.

*The First Pattern*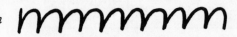

This pattern is very important for good writing and is fundamental to all styles

Although the youngest children are unlikely to achieve this pattern at all accurately for a long time, it is vital for the *teacher* to understand what is being aimed at.

Remember that child development is not a waiting for abilities to unfold, but the response of an active, physical creature to encouragement and examples given. Imitation and play are of equal value in growth. With the development of a specific skill like handwriting, imitation is very important. The teacher therefore has a duty to understand very fully the models and patterns that are set before the child. For this reason it will be of great help to the teacher to study an analysis of this first handwriting pattern.

Its shape is somewhat like the tail fin of an old fashioned aeroplane. It is useful to ask the children what they think the shape is like and to use their ideas in discussion, as they are more likely to remember their own perceptions.

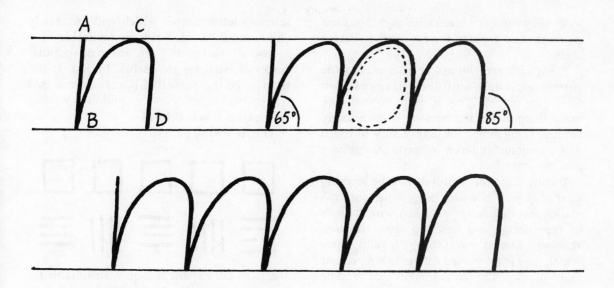

Starting at A, the line slopes at an angle of about 85 degrees to the writing line. From the writing line at B the line slopes up at an angle of about 65 degrees to a gentle curve at C and descends to D on a line parallel with AB. The line then springs up again like a bouncing ball at the 65 degree angle and so on.

The ideal pattern is not easy at first. It is subtle, and leans very slightly to the right, containing an oval shape as shown by the dotted line. Left handed children may find that their writing hand obscures what they are doing. In this case, their paper should be twisted to the right e.g.

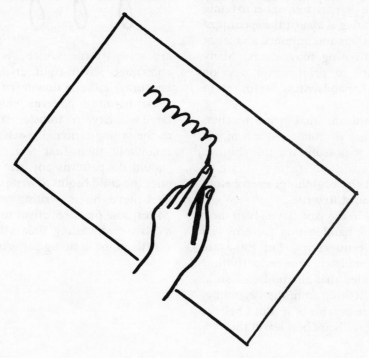

With very young children it helps to tape their paper to their desks in the easiest position for them.

Many children will not be able to copy the pattern accurately until they have practised for a year or two. This is quite normal. The main thing is for teachers to know exactly what is being aimed for, and gently to coach and encourage children towards this pattern and the others.

During this time, children will be learning to read as well as write. Long experience has shown that they adapt very easily to all kinds of type design and lettering styles in their reading. Almost everything around them which they learn to read differs in size, colour and legibility. The old argument that to write in print script was necessary because it was similar to their reading books is therefore not strictly true. However we do know that the first letter shapes which a child *writes for himself*, and those early habits of forming letters, are extremely important. What a child constructs for himself is learnt thoroughly. For this reason it is important that his first writing movements should be those handwriting movements which we wish him or her to retain for a lifetime. Printing is almost the *opposite* of writing. It is laborious and unjoined and is not done with handwriting movements. Many infants who learn to print script develop serious problems in handwriting for the rest of their school days.

Marion Richardson, that wise teacher, wrote in 1935 'that rhythmic pattern movements . . . make it possible for the child to experience the *essentially cursive nature of handwriting* from the beginning, even before he has actually learnt to write'.

Many teachers in the past have given their children rhythmic handwriting patterns *and* taught them to print script. But these are essentially two completely opposed activities!

It is not suggested that all children should be taught joined writing from the beginning, although many are capable of it. But I believe that handwriting skills are best learnt through learning letter shapes which will join easily and naturally as soon as it is practicable.

Not all patterns given in some popular books on writing are useful. Indeed, it has been found that some traditional patterns used by teachers actually make children's writing worse than it was before!

The following patterns

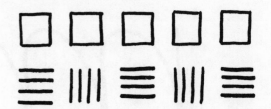

are, from my experience, quite unsuitable for encouraging good writing, and especially

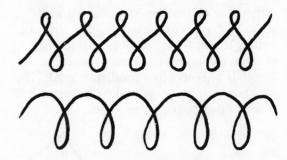

are all patterns which, while they may encourage left-to-right orientation, do not encourage either a flowing or a legible hand.

Furthermore, patterns which are done too large will have no transfer value or relevance to the young writer. Pre-school children and infants in their first few weeks at school should do patterns any size they wish. But once the child begins to write words, or at least to believe he is writing words, then the patterns he practises ought to be *the same size as his normal writing*. Unless this is done, there is little point in doing patterns at all.

*The Second Pattern*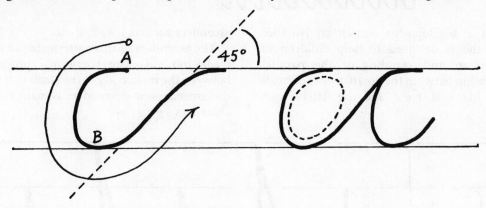

Individual teachers must decide for them-selves when to introduce this pattern as it is quite difficult; but the family of seven letters related to it are so vital that they, at least, must be learnt early on.

The pattern begins with a short horizontal stroke at A which then curves gently down almost to the writing line at B. The stroke then curves as part of an oval path touching the writing line, and slants up at an angle of about 45 degrees to make the ligature (join). Take the line a little way along the horizontal until the next point A is reached. The whole movement is then repeated to make the pattern.

It is important to stress that the shape contained within this *C* pattern is a forward-sloping oval or egg shape as shown by the dotted line in the diagram.

*The Third Pattern*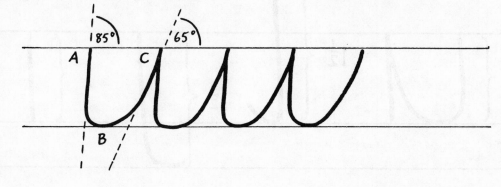

Pattern Number Three is really Number One upside down, but children should not be encouraged to turn their paper upside down and repeat Pattern One. The whole point of this exercise is to establish an anti-clockwise schema in the child's hand and mind. Like the first pattern, this one has a subtle shape which descends from A to B at an angle of about 85 degrees to the writing line and, curving gently, rises at a shallower angle ending up at about 65 degrees to the writing line.

Then the pen or pencil changes direction suddenly at C, without stopping or being lifted from the paper, and descends once more at an angle of 85 degrees.

*The Fourth Pattern*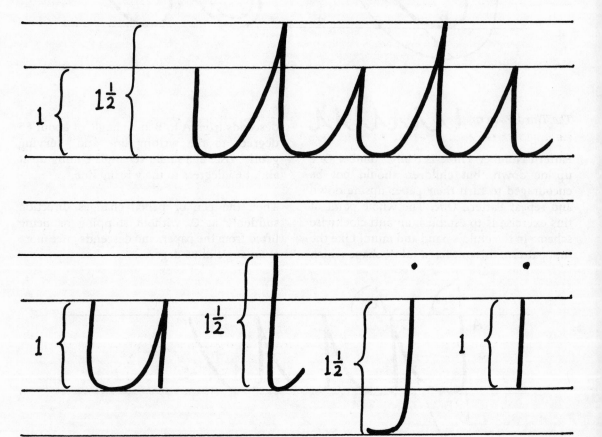

This pattern consists of two slanting rows of *parallel* strokes, and unless this is pointed out to pupils they (and perhaps the teacher too) may never notice it. The pattern is best started on a downstroke as V and W should be, and taken from left to right across the page. The lines should all slope at about 60 degrees either to the right or to the left. Keep the height of each peak even and *the same height as patterns 1, 2 and 3.*

---

*The Fifth Pattern*

This is a development of pattern Number Three and is designed to help children to develop an understanding of the parallel relationship between the downstrokes of small letters like i, u, t etc. and the letters with ascenders such as l, k, h, d etc.

The ascenders in this pattern should not be made too tall. The traditional proportion between the main body of the small letters and the ascenders or descenders is main body 1: ascenders 1½ e.g.

28

*The Sixth Pattern*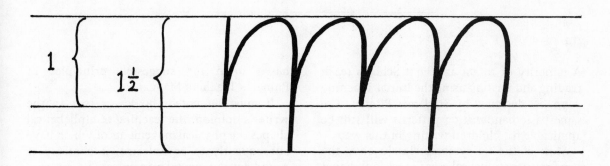

This pattern has a similar aim to Pattern Five, that is to help emphasize the parallel nature of the downstrokes in writing, while still practising the oval clockwise movement of Pattern Number One. In this pattern, the relative proportion of the descenders are being perceived and should be pointed out by the teacher, 1 to $1\frac{1}{2}$.

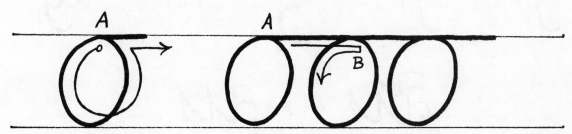

*The Seventh Pattern* OOOOOOO

This pattern is built upon the same forward-sloping oval as Pattern Two. It represents the shape of the main bodies of the letter family

c o a d g q e

and gives practice in the horizontal ligatures used with the letters

σ v w f t & r

The pattern starts at A with a short horizontal stroke to the left which gently curves down towards the writing line to form the oval. The line is brought in a curve back up to A and then taken in a long horizontal ligature to the next starting point. As each σ begins with a horizontal stroke from right to left, the ligature needs to be long enough for this return stroke to be made partially along it, as shown at B.

Although fairly obvious, teachers should use this opportunity to talk about *parallel* down-strokes. Some may not wish to use this particular term, but the acquisition of a new word will aid perception and the subsequent understanding of the concept. The pattern should be made from the left hand side of the page by downward strokes of alternating height. The slope should be about 85 degrees and parallel to the downstroke in Pattern One. Teach the children to look back to previous strokes when pattern making, in order to match their heights and slope.

---

### ita

A minority of Infant and First Schools teach reading and writing using the Initial Teaching Alphabet designed by Sir James Pitman. The same basic handwriting patterns will still be applicable for children writing in this way.

Most of the ita symbols clearly obey the same constructional rules as the basic alphabet described in the following pages. However, there are some symbols which might present difficulty. Reproduced below are recommended ways of constructing these. They are based upon the suggested principles in Pitman's Teachers Manual.

It must be noted, however, that in the writer's opinion, the teaching of alphabetical shapes the physical movements of which have subsequently to be unlearnt, is contrary to sound developmental principles. The 'success' of *ita* must owe more to teacher enthusiasm and the marvellous adaptability of children than to its merits as a medium.

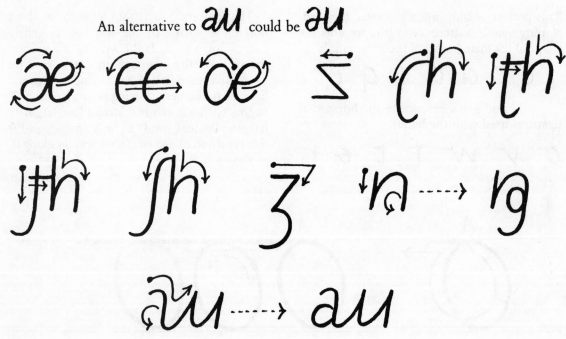

30

# A Basic Modern Hand

Without the slightest doubt the primary cause of illegibility in present-day handwriting is a lack of knowledge of the basic construction of the alphabet.

Reginald Piggott in
*Handwriting a National Survey* 1958

*What is a Basic Modern Hand?*

A Basic Hand is the simplest form of alphabet which can be written by hand without any extra loops, flourishes or conceits. It must be both legible and economical. The letter shapes need to be traditional rather than novel for legibility, and skeletal and speedy in order to be economical.

It should be plain and unobtrusive in character, so that having been acquired by any individual as a basic hand, it may be developed in character and personality to suit the writer.

It should not require any special inks, pens, pencils or papers, but be able to be written with, and upon any modern medium.

A basic modern hand must be capable of being learnt by the youngest children from the start of their education, without the basic forms or hand movements having to be changed at any later stage right up to the development of their mature adult handwriting.

It would be an enormous help to all children if a massive campaign were launched to encourage toy manufacturers to avoid using capital letters on children's toys and bricks, and to ask parents and playgroups to stop using capital letters too. Teaching little children to print their names in *capitals* retards their handwriting later on. There is a mistaken impression that capitals are easier to read than lower case. It is not true. In fact they tend to look more alike than the small letters. The Road Research Council established the fact that lower case letters are more legible some years ago, and that is why all road signs are now printed in lower case for speedier recognition by motorists.

*Stage One*

a b c d e f g h i j k l m n
o p q r s t u v w x y z

a b c d e f g h i j k l m n

o p q r s t u v w x y z

*Stage Three, joined where appropriate only*

abcdefghijklmn

opqrstuvwxyz

*The Capital Letters*

A B C D E F G H I J K L M N

O P Q R S T U V W X Y Z

## Teaching the Letter Families

Good copybooks provide good models but, with children, good models do not necessarily produce good writers – good teachers are the link.

Miss Margaret Browne
quoted by Alfred Fairbank in
*A Handwriting Manual* 1961 Edition

Although the basic handwriting patterns have been described in a separate section, they should not be thought of as coming solely *before* the letters. The relevant patterns need to be taught and practised *alongside* the letter families. Children need to come back to these fundamental patterns again and again, year after year. I have found that children who were excellent writers at the age of eight, may have quite forgotten the patterns and principles of good writing by the age of twelve.

There are other children, nevertheless, who have been keen, interested and encouraged all their school lives.

We will deal with the two main letter families first as they contain thirteen letters between them, exactly half of the alphabet.

Below are the patterns and the groups of letters which relate to them. Naturally some letters such as *i* and *l* correspond to more than one pattern.

| *Pattern* | *Value of Pattern* |
|---|---|
| mmmm | rnmhpbk |
| ccccc | coadgqe |
| uuuuuu | iuylt |
| wwwww | vwx |
| ишишиш | iuyltad |
| mmmm | rnpmh |
| ooooooo | co oo oa og od |
| ililililil | ilumh |

33

## 1. The First Family of Letters rnmhbp

The teacher should be very familiar with the shape of Pattern One and should write it on a blackboard, overhead projector, or on a sheet of paper pinned to an easel while the pupils watch. Whichever method you choose will depend upon the size of group involved and upon your own teaching style. Teachers of very young children, or of older remedial groups, may find it more suitable to make the pattern on a child's own book or sheet of paper in front of him. In general, however, the traditional blackboard and chalk is the most successful, and if a modern class is unused to this, the novelty will have greater impact!

As you write the pattern, explain where you are starting and finishing each curve and straight line, and ask the children to call out their own ideas of the shape. Some will say 'arches' or 'teeth', 'fingertips' or 'aeroplane tails'! Accept all suggestions, as it is their own

perceptions which they will remember, particularly if they have formulated them in words. When teaching the other patterns use the same method; but it is wise not to teach more than one family and its pattern in one day. Even in one week, two families can become confused. It is better to make each pattern and its related letters a separate experience for the children, spaced well apart in time. Then return continually to each pattern for revision purposes as required.

Next, ask the children which letters they can see hidden in the pattern. Some will say V and i or u. Treat such answers kindly, but say that those letters will be found in another pattern another day! When someone calls out 'n' or 'm' etc., praise them, and write the letter on the blackboard exactly the *same size and slope as the pattern*. Gradually build up the collection or family

rnmhbp

With older children, say eight years or over, one can add k to this family. With the youngest it is better to teach the shape k to begin with, as so many have not yet developed enough motor control to write k with a small loop. (Hence they will mostly write R and consequently confuse it with capital R.)

The teacher can now point out the family likeness of this group of letters. Unless this is quite consciously done, children (and many adults) are unlikely to notice it. One way of emphasising this family likeness is to draw each letter on top of the other, using a different coloured chalk each time i.e.

The next step is to ask the class to suggest words made up of letters from this family. They have not learnt any vowels in this lesson, of course, but it is likely that they have already been doing plenty of writing. One can perhaps use the letters i and o . Examples might be

# him pin prim
# mop bib rip

The aim of this exercise is to practise making the minims the same height and the down-strokes parallel. The most common difficulty at this stage is for children to achieve letters of even height. There is a strong temptation either to rule a top guideline for them, or to give them two lines to write between e.g.

# him moron

*This should be resisted*. Like so many apparently easy ways, it has drawbacks. An important part of the learning process at this stage is for children themselves to observe the even height of the small letters. Then each child must, through his own intentions and will, make the effort to achieve evenness in his writing. If this part is done for him mechani-

cally, it is equivalent to learning to walk by being given crutches. When the crutches are taken away, he is no further forward developmentally than the day on which he was given the crutches. It is by their own efforts, with merely the essential aid from adults, that children truly learn. A single supporting line to write on is sufficient.

## 2. The Second Family of Letters *coagdqe*

The teacher should be well acquainted with Pattern Two, and able to draw it for the children to watch. The essentially egg-shaped or oval nature of the main body of each letter should be pointed out.

In this case the joined pattern is probably harder than the letter shapes, and for this reason it may be better to concentrate on the letter group and leave the pattern until the diagonal joins are being taught. If you do not think the pattern is difficult, it is suggested that you study it again more closely! The more the teacher can train his or her own perceptions, the greater is the profit to the children.

(1) Starting with the letter *C*, begin at the top right at A and make a short horizontal stroke from right to left.

(2) Gently curve down at B. Here I find that the children remember this shape if I compare it to half a Christmas pudding!

It may sound ridiculous but it works.

(3) Curve fairly sharply near the writing line at C, but do not make it a V shaped corner, and leave the upward line at D pointing towards the starting point A.

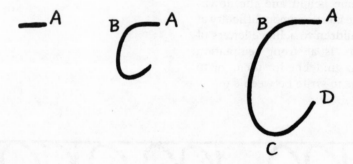

You may have to draw several large versions of this letter on the blackboard and encourage children to draw large ones too in their books.

Let them label their shape A, B, C, D, and talk about it. Eventually you will be rewarded with some rows of very nice *C* s.

CCCCCCC

This may take several weeks with some youngsters but no worthwhile skill is ever learnt instantaneously.

Do not concentrate only upon the *C* shape however. It is best to deal with the complete family together in the same lesson. Show immediately how the

*a g d q*

are formed by adding on to the first *C* shape. Then letter *e* is also the same shape, begun a little lower down to form the counter.

Once again you can draw with coloured chalks, one letter on top of another to show the family likeness.

Do not exaggerate the lengths of the ascenders and descenders. Remember they are traditionally half the length of the minim height. Also do not exaggerate the small flick at the end

of the descender of *q* . This letter, being

formed originally from the pictogram of a monkey ⚲ which became the Roman *Q* , has only one 'tail' and is formed either as *Q* or *q* .

I have found over many years that small children are less inclined to confuse it with the letter *p* or the number *q* if the little flick is added. It can also be considered as the last vestige of the extra ligature added by the eighteenth century copper engravers.

As with the other family of letters, ask the pupils to think of simple words made from this group of letters with which to practise. The children will always think of plenty but here are some standby examples.

# dog cad cog cage code

### 3. *The Third Letter Family* i u y t l

This is the only other main family and is related to Patterns Number Three and Six. As with the first family, I find it most helpful to write the third pattern on the blackboard or projector while the children watch. Comments and discussion are then invited. The slight forward slope is pointed out and the partially oval shape of the spaces noted. The parallel nature of the downstrokes is discussed and

then the 'family' of letters drawn out from the class and practised in their books. (If I do not go into step-by-step detail for each lesson, it is because, through observing many hundreds of teachers in the course of my own work, I know that one teacher cannot 'programme' another! It is always more efficient to give a teacher the facts; and her own interaction with a particular class will provide the detailed method.)

Once again I find that superimposing the family one upon the other helps to point out their similarity.

At this point it can be helpful to show children that all the following descenders are the same shape and size.

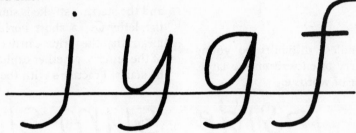

*The Rest of the small letters*

The letter f may be taught as this basic f , or with the flourished descender f . There is historical precedent for both forms. The main considerations are that the curves should not be exaggerated f f , and the straight back should be written parallel to the rest of the letters e.g.

flflflflf

Children nearly all find this letter difficult, along with s and k , due to the fine motor skills necessary to control these little curves. A very common fault is that of writing f leaning backwards ʂ . This error is sometimes

the result of practising a poor pattern:

The cross strokes of both f and t should be made at the height of the minims u m n etc. as they will eventually become fast economical joins e.g.

fi to fu ta

39

*Small l and capital I*

At this stage the l* is taught with a small serif or hook in order to distinguish it from the capital I which should be written as a single down-stroke l . The teaching of I as a kind of T.V. antenna on its side ⊥, is to be discouraged, as it is not an economical basic shape nor, historically, should those serifs be so exaggerated. One stroke is surely better than three. (This letter ⊥ is actually an early form of Z.)

s S

The S gives endless difficulty to young children and is very often written too large, even in the middle of words e.g.

aSk , inSide

The reason for this is twofold. Firstly, children (and perhaps some teachers!) do not perceive that the classical shape of the s, both small and capital, is based upon near horizontal strokes at the top and bottom e.g.

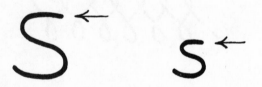

Historically, remember, this letter is descended from the Greek ⤨ which was formed with straight lines. Many children, through looking at print script and other forms perceive the s as a double circular shape S . Indeed it has taken this form at various stages in its history e.g. the Versal S and English half uncial S. Secondly, when attempting to write

a too-circular s young children will naturally tend to start with a vertical push upwards↖ . Being inexperienced, most misjudge the distance needed to complete the letter and end up with an s that is too high.

It is a help to children, therefore, to show them that s is more like two U shaped units lying on their sides, i.e.

and the starting stroke is similar to the start of the letter C , a short horizontal push. This means that the writer can decide the upper size of the letter s, whether capital or small, before he starts. Practise s with the minims e.g.

sum sisins

in order to emphasise the even height.

z

The letter zed or zee is a simple three-line design based on the Roman capital. The sixteenth century flourished version was z . The other tailed versions sometimes used as an alternative in the eighteenth century were ʒ and ȝ but although quite legible, they cannot be considered as part of a *basic* alphabet.

z needs to be practised with other minims too.

znznznzn
zuzuzuzu

---

*The historical reason for this form is in the table on page 104.

## Three Rules for Good Writing

Teaching good handwriting is a continuous, rather circular process. At each successive stage in the child's development he needs to be re-introduced to the basic patterns, shapes and skills involved. It does not matter how many times he has earlier been shown such skills. Learning does not take place once and for-ever in a sequence. Any physical skill such as handwriting has to be retraced and refined over and over again. We do not question the necessity for the concert pianist to spend hours on scales and arpeggios; nor should we neglect to encourage the practice of basic patterns and letter structures with children learning to write well.

True ease in writing comes from art[1] not chance
As those move easiest who have learned to dance.

The most neglected part in promoting the improvement of handwriting skills is the development of keen perceptions, in the children and the teacher. Unless both parties understand clearly what shapes, sizes, pro-portions etc. they are aiming at, then vague hopes for better writing will achieve nothing.

I have found that posing contrasts between good work and bad is a great help to all.

Three fundamental rules for good writing are:
1. To start and finish each letter in the correct place.
2. Each family of letters should be the same height.
3. All downstrokes must be parallel.

These three rules applied to any style of writing will result in an immediate improve-ment in its legibility and appearance. To ram home the point, however, it is important to demonstrate on blackboard, whiteboard or overhead projector what these rules mean. Of course a little humour always helps in this kind of example although I would not dare to prescribe my own feeble brand for others.

*Rule 1.* Write two lines of writing very obviously on the board. Label one A and the other B. By means of a little clowning, and obvious difficulty, form the letters in line A by starting in the wrong places. Show how hard it is to join an h to a u if both are formed from right to left. Then on line B form the letters rather obviously correctly. Ask the group which line is the correct one. To those wags who will inevitably call out line A I commend your professional skill.

*Rule 2.* Write two lines labelled A and B again. This time make the letters in one line all different sizes e.g.

A. The five boxing wizards

B. The five boxing wizards

Ask the children again which line is best. Most will say line B. One or two who say A, or who cannot tell which, should be noted for later study. I have found that some children's perception of blackboard writing is extremely unrefined even at age nine or ten, and some personal help in understanding what you are demonstrating is needed. There will also be some children whose language development is slow, and who have not really understood the question.

[1]Art here means skilled work as in artisan.

*Rule 3.* Use the same idea. Compare two lines labelled A and B (or X and Y for a change) and write one sentence with higgledy-piggledy slopes and one with careful parallel down-strokes:

A. *Pack my box with jugs*

B. *Pack my box with jugs*

It is rather important in these examples to show only one rule at a time in order to explain what you mean. In writing the sentences for Rule 3, therefore, try to keep each letter the same size!

## Children with Handwriting Difficulties

Before deciding that a child is having hand-writing difficulties it is important that the teacher should become familiar with the *normal* development of children's writing at different ages and stages. To help in this, some examples of ordinary children's standards at various ages are illustrated on page 10.

I have had several children referred to me by anxious parents because of their alleged poor handwriting. On meeting the child I have found that it is once again a ten year old who writes like a ten year old, whereas the adult was expecting him to write like an adult. This unfair expectation is not only frustrating for the adult, but creates a very poor atmosphere for further learning by the child. Very many children are criticised for poor handwriting when frankly it is their teacher who should be criticised for not taking firm steps to help the pupils. In my view it is quite unprofessional for a teacher to write on a child's work a comment such as 'You must improve your writing' unless the teacher is prepared to remedy the faults by teaching it herself. In handwriting, a child cannot, as it were, lift himself up by his own bootstraps. Unless the child is shown what is meant by good writing

and guided into how to achieve it, no amount of complaint or exhortation is going to help him.

Fortunately help is easy. Using only the Three Rules for Good Writing described on pages 41–42 any teacher can improve both her own writing, and her pupils' within a week. Within six months any class could be winning handwriting prizes. I do not make this claim lightly as I have been judging children's writing from all over Britain for the past ten years, and have seen great improvements take place in many schools through following the rules.

Children who do have genuine difficulty with their writing form a much smaller group than those having reading difficulties. Some quite illiterate children can copy writing very neatly, although unable to read. By this means in the past, many poorly-run schools were able to claim spuriously high standards. Children copied long passages neatly into their exercise books yet they could not understand one word.

The most important factor in overcoming writing difficulties is undoubtedly the relationship between the teacher and pupil. Warmth and affection and a great deal of patient encouragement will help the child most. Next, the detailed step-by-step explanation of how to draw the lettershapes and patterns. Allow the child in difficulty to regress back to the earliest stage of learning to write and bring him very gradually forwards again. With very retarded children, take them right back to the pre-school activities, tactile experiences and simple pencil manipulation tasks as described on page 16. Some children love to use chalk on the blackboard. Even at secondary school age this can be most beneficial. Painting handwriting patterns on large sheets, and making handwriting movements in the air to music can also help. I have found that putting on a rhythmic Mozart or Vivaldi record during remedial handwriting classes establishes a wonderful atmosphere for learning to write. Hawaiian music is also very effective!

With children whose handwriting level is well below their age level, there is always an emotional problem and most teachers today will take that for granted. Very often there is a physical problem too. This may be a slight spasticity which is congenital; but even very clumsy children, given the will to succeed, will produce legible writing with practice. I have found that with severe physical difficulties such as this, an unjoined script is more easily achieved, since the pupil can concentrate on one letter at a time. With perceptual problems or cross laterality (i.e. when a child is right eye and left hand dominant or vice versa) perseverance and practice with shape matching and tracing will increase their skills.

I recommend the use of acres of tracing paper to help children with difficulties. Provided they are started off well, and shown which way to begin each letter or pattern, tracing is an excellent activity because it is self-correcting for the learner. I also recommend most strongly the use of mazes and numbered dot-to-dot pictures. Do not allow your conscience to worry about the non-creative aspect of such work. Children in severe difficulties are longing to be creative. These seemingly dull activities provide a real challenge for the less able and will become the platform for creative work in the future.

Children with perceptual problems often find it hard to transfer their eyes from long sight on a blackboard or screen to short sight on a book or paper close to them. For most remedial work a personal copy sheet or workcard is best. But remember a child will not *learn* to write from a workcard or copybook. The teacher must teach the shapes and movements personally in the first place. The worksheet is strictly for revision only, and *after* the learning has taken place.

## Awkward Penholds and Left Handers

Once a child is over nine years old it is not easy to change his pen hold. Any magic formula for achieving this which a reader has found will be gratefully acknowledged. It is possible to stick a pencil through a lump of plasticine or self-hardening clay and to mould a correct finger hold for an individual. (Pyruma Fire Cement, made by Purimachos Bristol Ltd. and stocked by most hardware stores is suitable.) If one has a plastic casting facility, a permanent pencil grip could be made.

The amount of clay used will depend on the size of the child's hand. When the ball of soft clay is on the pencil, take the child's hand and close it for him over the clay so that it squeezes into a moulded shape. The child must allow you to place his hand and fingers in the normal pencil grip position for him. That is, with the pencil held between his thumb and middle finger and the forefinger on top to steady it.

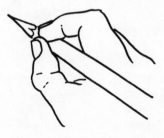

The fire cement will harden overnight if left in a warm place. Then, when the pupil comes to grip the mould and pencil, he can only comfortably hold it in the correct way. After a week or two the new habit is formed.

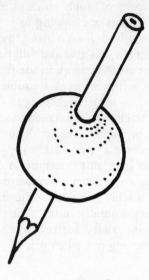

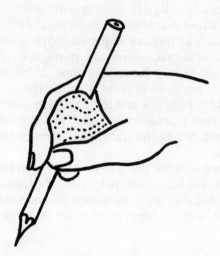

Left handers can often be helped by tilting their book or paper to the right.

Encourage left handers to sit on the left end of double desks or tables to give them more arm room. From an early age the left hander should be shown how to hold his pencil or pen with the handle pointing back up his arm towards his left shoulder.

right

If he is allowed to hold the pencil with its back pointing away above the writing line, a poor posture and poor pen control will result. The left hander is tempted to take up these positions in an effort to see his own work. Because

wrong

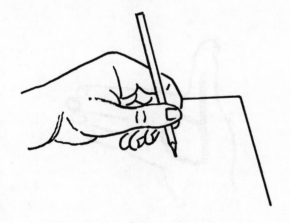

our writing system is a right handed one, without help, the left handed writer obscures his own work. Every teacher should spend a little time writing with her left hand in order to gain some insight into the problem.

Some left handers are certainly helped by the special left handed nibs which are supplied by Osmiroid Educational and by Platignum Pens. These nibs are either cropped at an oblique angle to the left

or manufactured with a bend to the left.

If an older left hander is given one of these nibs, he or she may have quite a lot of adjustment to make in order to get used to it. But left handed younger children, given these nibs on their first introduction to pen and ink writing, find them very helpful indeed.

## Reversal of Letters

The reversal of certain letters by some children may persist well after their seventh year; in particular letters such as p, q, b, d, j, e, and sometimes g. Recent research by Dr. Robert Zazlow has found that the problem may be solved if children are helped to be made aware of their own body midline.

They should then be encouraged to write the difficult letter by reaching from their normal writing position across their midline to write that letter. This simple act of crossing the midline of their own torso seems to set up the necessary orientation to eliminate reversals in many cases.

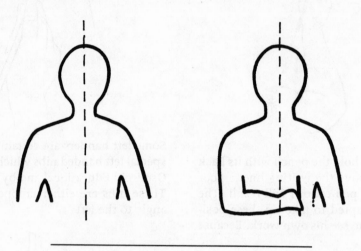

I have also found it a great help to write say, d on the back of a child's left hand and thumb, and b on the back of his right hand and thumb

(with a ballpoint). We then call the left hand 'Daddy's hand' and the right hand 'Baby's hand'.

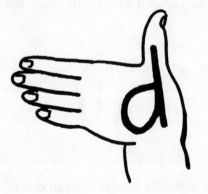

# The Copy Pages

The following set of copy sheets may be reproduced by any process by teachers for use in their own schools. Multiple copies may not be made without the permission of the publishers. These pages may not be reproduced in any other publication without permission of the publisher.

The prime purpose of writing is to be read. The Penman is a Craftsman. His direct objective is to write well. Writing well, for him, means making good use of his pen and his alphabets: it means writing clear, 'true' pen-characters fitted for the particular purpose, use, or function of the thing he is making.

From Edward Johnston's *Formal Penmanship and Other Papers* ed. by Heather Child 1971

The copy pages are presented in three stages as follows.

*Stage 1*

*Copy pages 1–29* These are all the basic patterns and basic lettershapes including the capital letters and the numerals. This section forms the equivalent to the print script or manuscript stage given to the youngest children in the past.

*Stage 2*

*Copy pages 30–35* This is the vital link stage where the hooks or serifs are added to the basic letters in preparation for joining. Then the simple joins are shown.

*Stage 3*

*Copy pages 36–51* These show practice with joined handwriting and the change to using ink if desired.

Each stage should be introduced by the teacher on the blackboard or O.H. projector and the copy pages only used by the children individually for revision. Photocopies may be made and mounted on cards for this purpose if desired.

## Stage 1. Basic Modern Hand

### Copy page One

The first pattern. Trace or copy this as accurately as possible. Start at the dot and follow in the direction of the arrow. Patterns teach left to right movement and correct height and letter shape. These copy pages are for revision by children of shapes and movements already learnt from the blackboard or individually from the teacher.

## Copy page Two

The family of letters which is formed from the
first pattern. For the best results practise the
letters the same size and shape as the line of
pattern.

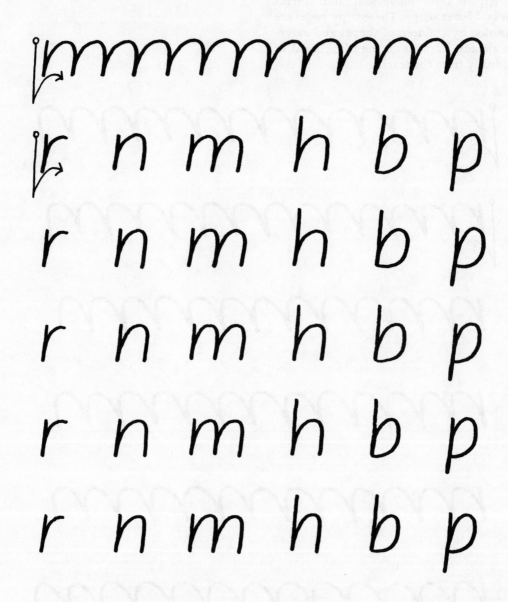

# Copy page Three

The second pattern. Trace or copy this as
accurately as possible.

## Copy page Four

The family of letters which is formed from the second pattern. The basic 'c' shape, shown large on this page, should be traced several times and its particular oval form memorised. Before copying this page, children should have had several lessons on it from the blackboard or overhead projector.

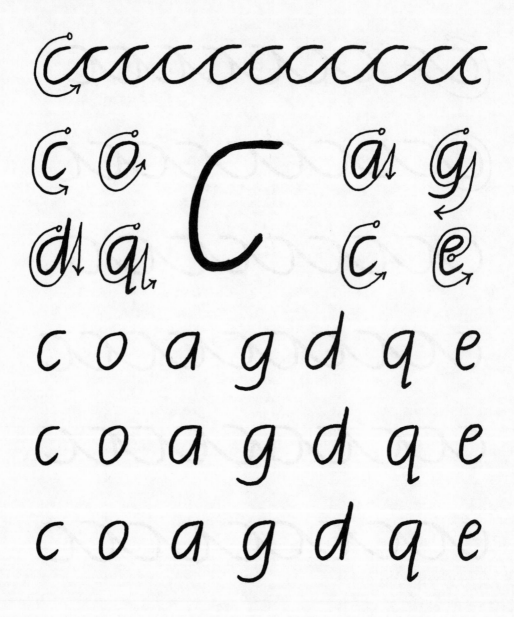

## Copy page Five

The third pattern. Trace or copy this as
accurately as possible.

# Copy page Six

The family of letters which is formed from the third pattern. Remember that the descender of the y is only half the length of the body of the letter. Letter t is not as tall as the letter l, and the crosspiece of t is at the height of the small letters.

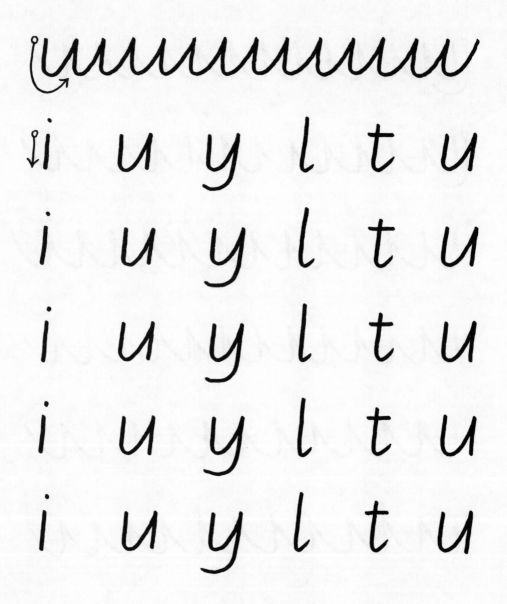

# Copy page Seven

The fourth pattern. Trace or copy this as accurately as possible. Remember each slope should be parallel to its similar neighbour.

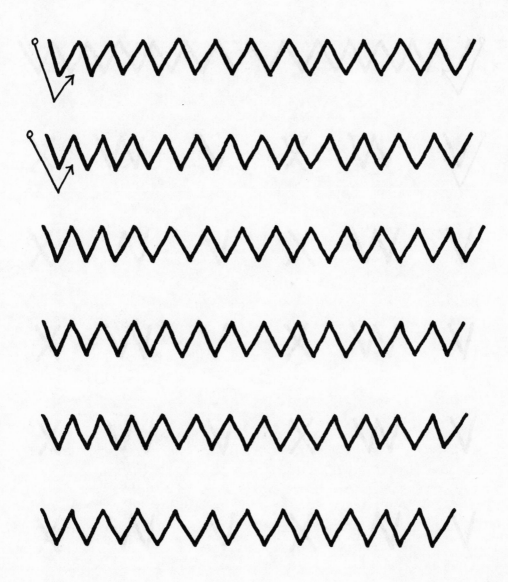

## Copy page Eight

The family of letters which is formed from the fourth pattern. Note that the centre point of w is of equal height to the arms. Letter x may be formed with either stroke first, whichever is preferred.

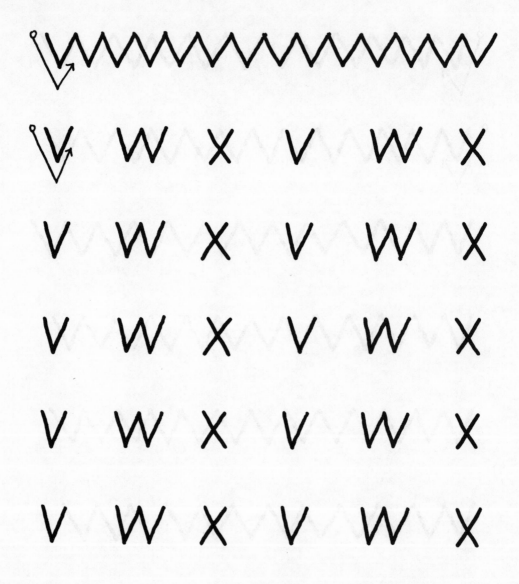

# Copy page Nine

The fifth pattern. This is to help children to understand the relative heights of the small letters and ascenders.

## Copy page Ten

The family of letters which is formed from the fifth pattern. Notice that many letters are alike in their design as well as differing in parts.

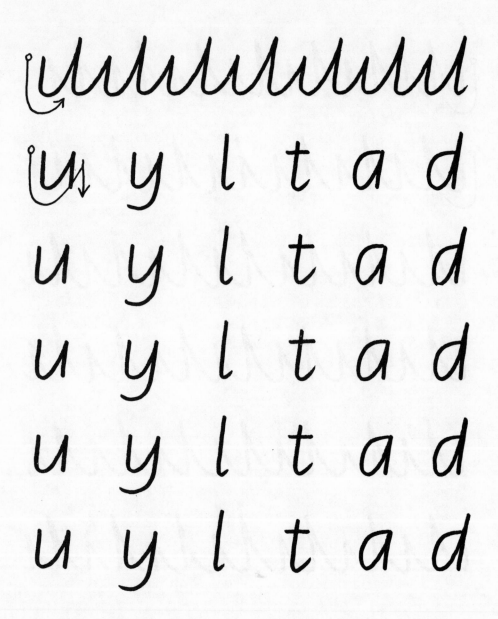

## Copy page Eleven

The sixth pattern. Trace or copy this as accurately as possible. It is to help in the awareness of the ratio of size between the small letters and the descenders.

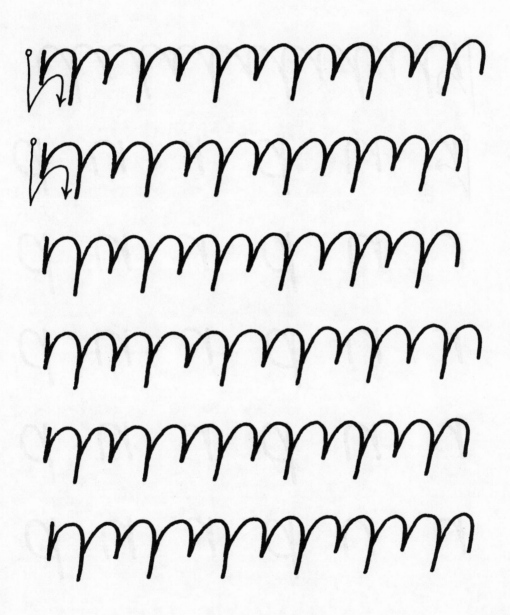

## Copy page Twelve

The family of letters which is formed from the sixth pattern.

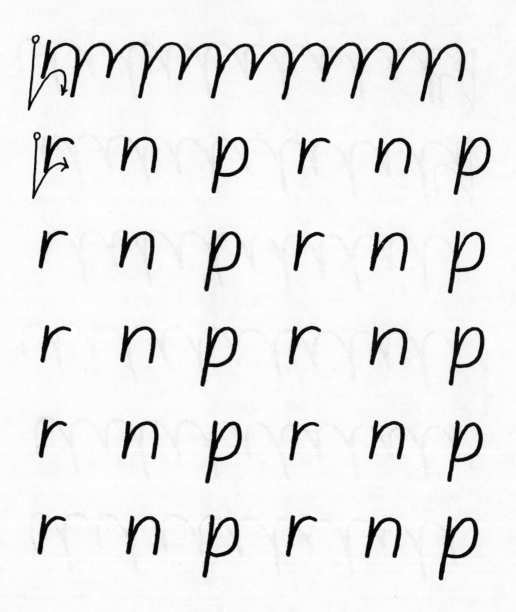

# Copy page Thirteen

The seventh pattern. Trace or copy this as
accurately as possible.

## Copy page Fourteen

The horizontal joins from the letter o, which
will be learnt later on, may be introduced here
if desired.

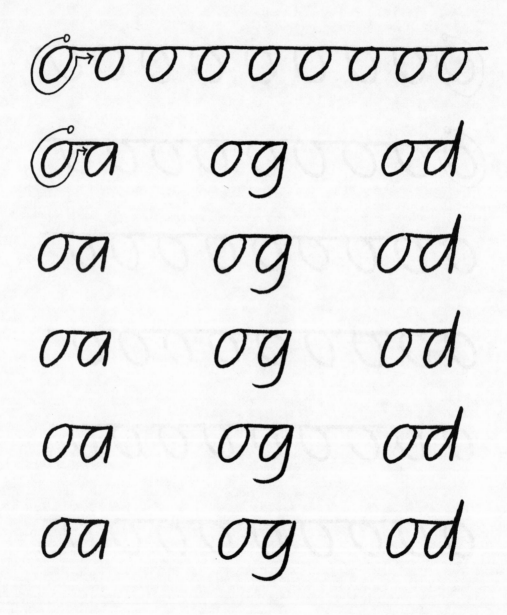

## Copy page Fifteen

The Eighth pattern. This is quite difficult to copy accurately. It provides more practice in parallel downstrokes and that important ratio between the height of small letters and the ascenders.

## Copy page Sixteen

Practice of the letter f. Note that it is parallel
with the m and that the cross stroke is at the
height of the m and n.

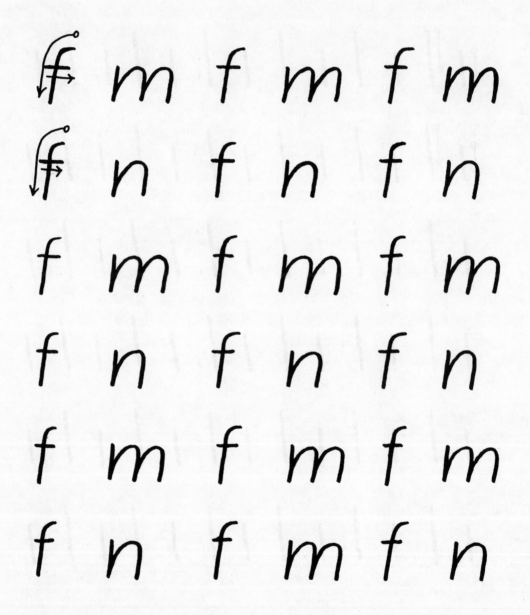

# Copy page Seventeen

More letter practice. Do not make the descender of j too curly or too long.

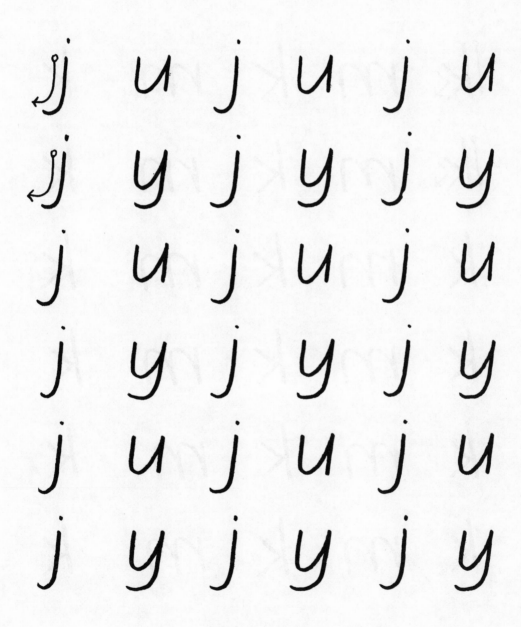

## Copy page Eighteen

Pratice for small letter k. The open k is
preferred for the younger learners to avoid
confusion with the capital R.

k m k m k

k m k m k

k m k m k

k m k m k

k m k m k

k m k m k

## Copy page Nineteen

Practice for small letters s and z. Notice how
the first stroke is horizontal for both these
letters.

Some words to copy. Can you make a sentence out of them? All 26 letters of the alphabet are here.

lazy quick fox

over jumps

dog brown

the lazy over

quick the brown

fox jumps dog

An alphabet sentence to copy. You will find
many others on page 101.

many big
jackdaws
quickly zipped
over the fox
pen

Another alphabet sentence.

the five mmm

boxing uuuu

wizards wwww

jump ooooo

quickly uuuuu

# Copy page Twenty-three

The numerals. Remember that all these are started at the top. Number 8 may be begun either clockwise or anticlockwise, whichever is preferred.

## Copy page Twenty-four

One-stroke capital letters. Capital M may also be formed in two strokes, starting at the top left if preferred.

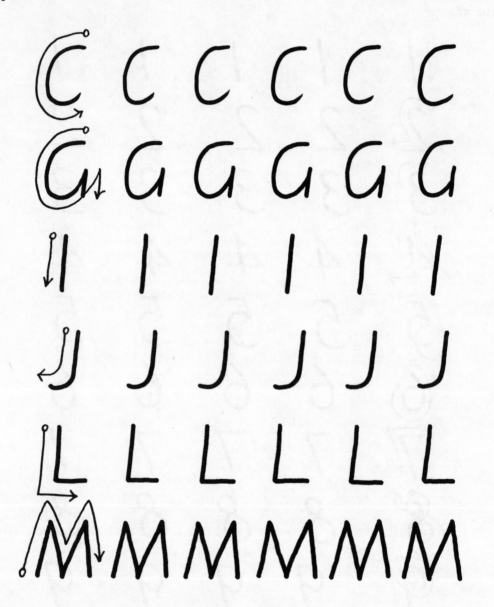

Roman Capitals are . . . 'the queen of all the alphabets . . . and he who can write Roman Capitals can write anything'.

Gianfrancesco Cresci, 1570.

'When in doubt, use Roman Capitals'.

Edward Johnston, 20th century.

# Copy page Twenty-five

One-stroke capital letters. Capital N may be
formed in two strokes, starting at the top left if
preferred.

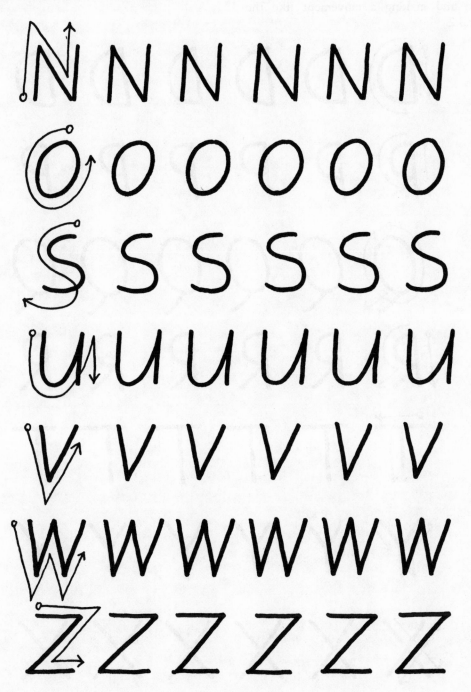

## Copy page Twenty-six

The two-stroke capital letters. Notice that the descender of Q does not pierce the circle. Q can also be formed in one stroke starting at the bottom and making a movement like the numeral 2.

# Copy page Twenty-seven

The three-stroke capitals.

Using capital letters: notice the relative heights of the capitals, the small letters and the ascenders.

# Alan Bob Colin

# Dale Eva Fay

# Geof Harry Ivor

# Jim Kate Linda

# Mary Nan Olga

# Pat Quentin

Roderick Sam
Thomas Una
Valerie Wayne
Xavier Yolande
Zebediah

| | | | | | | | | | | | | | | | | | | | | | | | |

## Copy page Thirty

Adding hooks: when you have learnt all the
letters and can write them neatly, you should
add the small hooks to make joins easier later
on.

$$a \; a \; a \; a \; a \; a$$

$$d \; d \; d \; d \; d \; d$$

$$h \; h \; h \; h \; h \; h$$

$$i \; i \; i \; i \; i \; i$$

$$k \; k \; k \; k \; k \; k$$

$$m \; m \; m \; m \; m \; m$$

**Copy page Thirty-one**

The hooks. These are properly called serifs, and should be sharply curved but not pointed. Do not make them too big. Serifs are added only where joins will be made.

The horizontal joins. Basically there are only two kinds of join or ligature. They are horizontal or diagonal. These horizontal joins occur with small letters that finish at the top of a stroke, such as o v w r t f.

from to worn

room on view

troop over fort

two fox wood

fun hoof ford

foot vote top

The diagonal joins. Use the joins to make even spaces between letters.

hide it came

dim my sun

main chain

do mum and

that has at

dig is his nip

The unjoined letters. It is sensible to leave some letters unjoined. They are usually b g j p q y and s. Copy these letters. The star shows where the natural breaks occur.

bath about able

again goat gap

jug jumble jam

put pig paper

queen question

you trying yolk

## Copy page Thirty-five

Alternative forms of letters. Traditionally there have always been variations in some basic letters. Six common alternatives are shown here. Note that the one-stroke d is best suited for the end of a word as it does not join naturally.

d    d    and odd

e    e    e even

f    f    for sniff

g    g    going

q    q    quick

s    s    as grass

**Copy page Thirty-six**

Joining practice.

an at bun bin can cap
dim din end eleven fun
fin gun game hum hop
inn imp jam jump kin
kill lump line mum my
nun nine one over pun
pin quince quick run rip
sun sing tan tin unto
under van vim won wave
you yonder zinc zebra
amamamamamamamamam

My Go Cart

Lucky me - I've got a go cart. I'm going to try it out. Give me a push off. Thank you very much.

Faster, faster and faster still! And everything goes blurred. We have started to slow down again. Slower, slower and slower still. And now we have stopped - everything seems to have stopped

Boy 7 years.

# Things I See Outside

Outside I can see
People, but they cannot see me.
Outside I can see
Washing out on the line,
But it cannot see me.

Outside I can see
Men on a digger,
But they cannot see me.
Outside I can see
Bricks, but they cannot see me.

Girl 8 years.

The Tractor

The tractor starts and its
mighty wheels turn
Purring then winding
up to a loud roar,
The engine oily & greasy
Chugging while it pauses,
Stones crunching under
its wheels,
Charging into a real speed,
Throwing up the earth,
Charging like a wild boar,
Then creeches to a jerky
stop.                    Boy 10 years.

THE HORRIFYING NIGHT
The most horrifying night
Is when the winds bite.
The frost lies on the ground
And the rain is falling down
Silence is worst,
Then suddenly a burst.
Enemies are attacking.
Bullets flying overhead,
This is the most horrifying
                    night.
              Elizabeth age 11.

The Reflection of a Ruin.
The rippling reflection of a
Ruin by a lake.
A desolate garrison
That waits for morning's
     break.

A silent breeze comes
Ripples the water,
While a king waits
For his daughter.
Then there's a battle
With hunger and strife.
And the castle that lived
Lost its life.   Boy 11 years.

USING A FOUNTAIN PEN

The rest of these copy sheets are meant to be used with a pen. The words can be copied or traced using any kind of nib. But in order to achieve the shaded calligraphic effect of the thick and thin lines, an italic or chisel nib is needed. Right handed writers should hold the pen so that the nib points to the left hand top corner of the page like this.

Keep the nib at this angle all the time you are writing. Now copy these patterns. Keep them the same size as on this page.

# Copy page Forty-three

Some pen patterns to trace or copy.

MWWWWWWWWWWWWWWWWW

ooooooooooooooooooooooo

ccccccccccccccccccccccc

cococococococococococ

amamamamamamama

bgbgbgbgbgbgbgbgbgbgb

ururururururururur

fmfmfmfmfmfmfmfmfm

wwwwwwwwwwwwwwwwwww

wowowowowowow

tntntntntntntntntnt

us us us us us us us us us us us

**Copy page Forty-four**

Pen capitals for good handwriting should be
based upon the plain Roman capitals.

A A A A    B B B B

C C C C    D D D D

E E E E    F F F F

G G G G    H H H H

I I I I    J J J J

K K K K    L L L L

M M M M    N N N N

## Copy page Forty-five

The pen capitals continued.

O O O O P P P P

Q Q Q Q R R R R

S S S S T T T T

U U U U V V V V

W W W W X X X X

Y Y Y Y Z Z Z Z

The Great War
The trenches are horrid
and dismal,
You wait all night fearing
death,
Men die, their bodies roll
in the mud,
Their bodies covered with
rubble,
Friends are blown to bits.
by Scott age 11

North Winds

Underneath the city spires
People hurry to their fires,
With quick paces
And raw faces.
The fingers of the leaden sky
Claw the clouds that scurry by.
North winds shriek
Over county bleak.
The leafless trees bow and sigh
For the birds that soon will die
Wolves prowl near
The frightened deer.

by Jonathan age 9.

# Autumn

Autumn's dying, winter's forming.
Winter's icy fingers are creeping
in. The wind is clawing, like a
lion pawing, soon in the fight,
cold will win and smoke will
pour from every chimney. The
fresh northerly wind gushing
in.

Leaves spiral from their homes.
The trees are going bald. The
sun shines like a light seen
shining in a pool, somehow
drowning in the cloudy sky
by Martyn age 10

Japanese SENRYU written
by 13 year old English children.

Pheasant
glides through the air,
A hang-glider.

A song-thrush
sings all day long
Sponsored sing-song.

A cat
cleans its fur
by machine.

The elephant
never forgets
A computer.

Piper, sit thee down and write
In a book that all may read!
So he vanished from my sight;
And I pluck'd a hollow reed.

And I made a rural pen
And I stained the water clear,
And I wrote my happy songs
Every child may joy to hear.

William Blake.

"On oval wheels should fair
Italian run
Smooth as the whirling
chariot of the sun."
Edward Cocker.

"With one sole pen I wrote this book
Made of a grey goose quill.
A pen it was when I it took
And a pen I leave it still."
Philomen Holland.
16th cent.

99

Many teachers, after years of familiarity with the childish scrawls of their pupils, seem to find genuine difficulty in acclimatizing themselves to a rational script. Italic can, of course, become 'ragged and vile' if it is not controlled; but this danger is not peculiar to Italic.

Wilfrid Blunt
In *Sweet Roman Hand*, published 1952

# Alphabet Sentences

It is expected that good handwriting practice will always be found in the work which arises out of children's current interests and projects. Now and again, in addition to this, teachers may want to emphasise a certain aspect of handwriting, such as letter size or ligatures. For those brief moments of teaching, sentences which contain all the letters of the alphabet are both useful and amusing. The best known has become such a cliché that many people may believe it to be the only alphabet sentence: 'The quick brown fox jumps over the lazy dog'. Over the years I have collected many more, and am indebted to Fred Eager, John L. Larkin, and Kenneth Hardacre for some of the following. The sentences which makes the least sense are often the most useful in teaching, as children have to look more carefully at the words!

The sentences have been listed in length order so that teachers of younger children may select the earlier ones in the list if they wish.

Some of the images posed by the zanier versions make for hilarity. The person who sticks in my mind, and whom I would love to meet, is Martin J. Hixeypozer. Who is he, and what does the 'J' stand for? A. S. Osley once wrote, 'Of course the real trick would be to compose a *palindromic* sentence which sounded natural, could be read both ways and did not rely much on exotic Christian names'. Any reader who succeeds, please share the result!

1. The five boxing wizards jump quickly.
2. Pack my box with five dozen liquor jugs.
3. Jail zesty vixen who grabbed pay from quack.
4. Dumpy kibitzer jingles as exchequer overflows.
5. Martin J. Hixeypozer quickly began his first word.
6. Brawny gods just flocked up to quiz and vex him.
7. Jim just quit and packed extra bags for Liz Owen.
8. Many big jackdaws quickly zipped over the fox pen.
9. A large fawn jumped quickly over white zinc boxes.
10. Five or six big planes zoomed quickly by the new tower.
11. The exodus of jazzy pigeons craved by squeamish walkers.
12. Now is the time for all brown dogs to jump over the lazy lynx.
13. The vixen jumped quickly on her foe barking with zeal.
14. Picking just six quinces, the new farm-hand proved strong but lazy.
15. Alfredo just must bring very exciting news to the plaza quickly.
16. Anxious Paul waved back his pa from the zinc quarry just sighted.
17. Venerable Will played jazz sax 'til 3 o'clock in the morning before he quit.
18. Travelling beneath the azure sky in our jolly ox-cart, we often hit bumps quite hard.
19. Someone just asking was quite pleased with our gifts of a zebra and a clever oryx.
20. As we explored the gulf of Zanzibar, we quickly moved closer to the jutting rocks.
21. Their kind aunt was subject to frequent dizzy spells, thus causing much anxiety and worry.
22. William said that everything about his jacket was in quite good condition except for the zipper.
23. The junior office clerks were quite amazed at the extra reward given by their generous employer.

The *Guinness Book of Records* gives the most unlikely example of an alphabet sentence. It is only interesting because the 'author' managed to use precisely the exact twenty six letters of the alphabet! It is meant to be a newspaper headline about the reaction of despicable vandals from the valley thwarted by finding a block of quartz with carvings on it: 'Quartz glyph job vex'd cwm finks'.

# Resources for Project Work

The next sections give the teacher some historical background which can be used as lesson notes or reference material depending upon the age of children being taught. Also, there are a number of activities which have been found of great interest to primary age children. Quill cutting and pattern making, decorated capital letters and so on are particularly popular.

In the writer's experience, cutting a quill and showing how man wrote for over two thousand years is the best way of starting an interest in writing. If some genuine parchment or vellum documents, such as old property deeds, can be brought into school, these will also lead to a keen interest. Following such practical activities, the historical information comes alive both for the pupils and the teacher. Even the youngest children enjoy such project work. A list of suitable references is given at the end of this book.

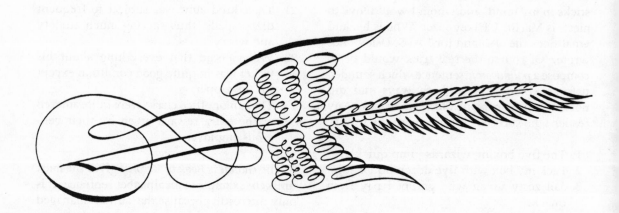

## Historical Development

Writing began as drawing. Most people have seen pictures of early cave paintings, and we are all familiar with signs which give us information, even today.

Opening bridge     Quayside or river bank

The Sumerians, who lived in what is now modern Iraq about five thousand years ago, seem to have been the earliest people to develop a written language. Their country had a great many marshes and swamps and so clay and reeds were common materials. A slab of clay made a flat surface for marking on, and a reed stalk with a triangular cross section was easily pressed into the clay. Signs which began as recognisable drawings of birds, fish or oxen at first, gradually became rather abstract, being formed from the wedge-shaped marks of the reeds. So these signs have now been called cuneiform writing, from the Latin word cuneus meaning a wedge.

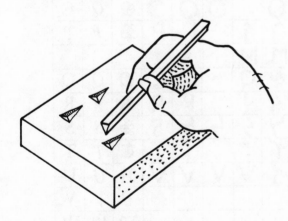

Using a triangular section reed stalk to make cuneiform writing marks.

This is how some of the original Sumerian pictures became cuneiform writing.

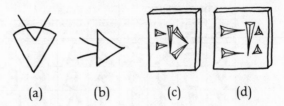

(a)     (b)     (c)     (d)

You can see how a simplified drawing of an ox head with horns (a) was copied by later scribes, sometimes upside down and sometimes on its side (b). Then later, the shape was copied (c) using the reed pressed into a clay tablet. Perhaps many years later, writers in clay copying the shape at (c) tidied it up, and the ox head has become an abstract sign (d).

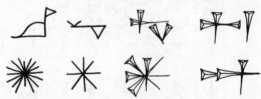

This kind of writing, where pictures or signs represent objects or complete ideas, is called LINEAR WRITING, and the signs are called PICTOGRAMS and IDEOGRAMS.

The trouble with pictograms is that a sign such as can mean bird (English) or Vogel (German) or oiseau (French) or it may be a swan or a chicken. There is no way of knowing *exactly* what it means, nor can we even know which language it is in. On the other hand a series of letters b-i-r-d, can only signify the English word bird. And the letters s-w-a-n signify the English word swan. It is easy to see how much more precise and useful an alphabet of letters can be than pictograms.

Scholars now generally believe that the Phoenician merchants some 3,500 years ago first developed an alphabet of twenty-two letters based upon Egyptian hieroglyphs. Hieroglyphs are a form of LINEAR WRITING. We can make a family tree of the development of present-day handwriting from Egyptian hieroglyphs.

| NORTH SEMITIC | | | | GREEK | | | | ETRUSCAN | | LATIN | | | MODERN CAPITALS | | |
|---|---|---|---|---|---|---|---|---|---|---|---|---|---|---|---|
| EARLY PHOENICIAN Late 2nd Millennium B.C. | CURSIVE EARLY HEBREW Later Letters | MOABITE c. 842 B.C. | PHOENICIAN c. 8th. Cent. BC | EARLY GREEK c. 6th. Cent. BC | EASTERN GREEK c. 6th Cent. BC | WESTERN GREEK c. 6th. Cent. BC | CLASSICAL GREEK 403 B.C. onward | MARSILIANA TABLET c. 8th. Cent. B.C. | CLASSICAL c. 600 B.C. | PRAENESTE FIBULA c. 7th. Cent. B.C. | MONU-MENTAL LATIN c. 1st. Cent. BC | CLASSICAL LATIN c. 4th. Cent. BC | GOTHIC | ITALIC | ROMAN |

(The body of the table consists of hand-drawn letterforms tracing the development of each letter across the columns listed above, culminating in the Modern Capitals A, B, C, D, E, F, G, H, I, J, K, L, M, N, O, P, Q, R, S, T, U, V, W, X.)

| CURSIVE MAJUSCULE | CURSIVE MINUSCULE | ROMAN UNCIALS | ROMAN SEMI-UNCIALS | ANGLO-SAXON MAJUSCULE | CAROLINE MINUSCULE | GOTHIC | VENETIAN MINUSCULE (ITALIC) | N. ITALIAN MINUSCULE ROMAN | MODERN LOWER CASE | | |
|---|---|---|---|---|---|---|---|---|---|---|---|
| | | | | | | | | | GOTHIC | ITALIC | ROMAN |

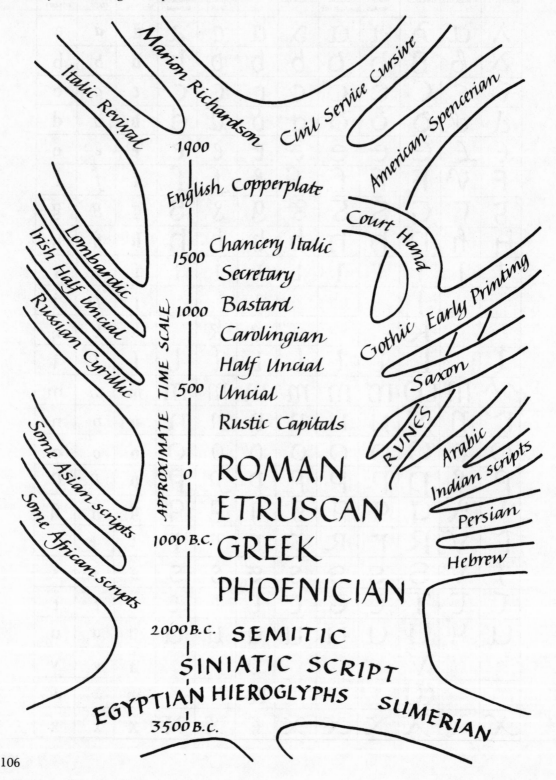

Marion Richardson

Civil Service Cursive

American Spencerian

Italic Revival

English Copperplate

Court Hand

Lombardic

Irish Half Uncial

Russian Cyrillic

1900

1500 Chancery Italic

Secretary

1000 Bastard

Carolingian

Half Uncial

500 Uncial

Rustic Capitals

Gothic Early Printing

Saxon

RVNES

Arabic

Indian scripts

Persian

Hebrew

APPROXIMATE TIME SCALE

Some Asian scripts

Some African scripts

0

ROMAN

ETRUSCAN

1000 B.C.

GREEK

PHOENICIAN

2000 B.C. SEMITIC

SINIATIC SCRIPT

EGYPTIAN HIEROGLYPHS

SUMERIAN

3500 B.C.

As well as the alphabet arising from Egypt and the Middle East, we must not forget that in parts of Northern Europe runic signs or 'runes' were developed to a high degree. 'Runic' means 'mysterious' and the signs in Scandinavian countries and in Britain were the secret writing of the old religious priesthoods. They formed a phonetic alphabet, but it may be assumed that the runes too could have arisen from pictograms in earlier days, as some of their shapes clearly indicate.

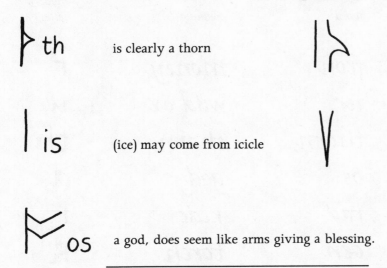

th     is clearly a thorn

is     (ice) may come from icicle

os     a god, does seem like arms giving a blessing.

---

However, this is only speculation. Thorn þ and wyn ƿ survived in Anglo Saxon writing until the Norman Conquest and then th and w superseded them. Perhaps our row of xxxxx as kisses at the end of a letter is a survival of the geofu x (gift)? It is more probable that the x is a Christ-cross or criss-cross used as a blessing. Runic writing was suppressed by the Romans in Britain as being part of an uncivilised, barbaric cult.

It is said the European runes probably arose from Etruscan writing. Certainly the signs below seem to come directly from the same source as the Greek and Roman forms. They may have been evolved for carving on wood rather than on stone. You will notice that there are no horizontal strokes which could have been obscured by the grainy wood fibres.

*Some Old English Runic Symbols (possibly 2nd Century B.C.)*

| symbol | word | meaning | modern letter |
|--------|------|---------|---------------|
| ᚠ | feoh | money | f |
| ᚢ | ur | wild ox | u |
| ᚦ | thorn | thorn | th |
| ᚩ | os | god | a |
| ᚱ | rad | ride | r |
| ᚳ | cen | torch | R |
| ᚷ | geofu | gift | g |
| ᚹ | wyn | joy | w |
| ᚻ | haegl | hail | h |
| ᚾ | nied | need | n |
| ᛁ | is | ice | i |
| ᛄ | gear | year | j |
| ᛇ | eoh | yew | e |
| ᛈ | peord | dance | p |
| ᛋ | secq | sedge | m |

# The Development of Informal Handwriting

Mainly due to the growth of the Roman Empire and subsequently of the Christian religion throughout Europe, more systems of communication became necessary. Books, letters, orders, legal documents and records became more frequent as civilisation spread.

Roman publishers worked by seating a slave on a high chair to read a manuscript aloud while up to a hundred slave scribes copied down the dictated book. In this way a hundred copies were made simultaneously. Errors were quite frequent from misheard words and phrases. It is interesting to compare these Roman *misheard* errors with the later medieval scribes' *misread* errors, showing that the later scribes copied books out individually rather than in the Roman mass-produced manner.

For fourteen hundred years after the birth of Christ books were written by hand and copied out by hand. They were written most often with goosewing quills, upon vellum which is calf skin, or the lighter weight parchment made from sheep or goat skin.

Other birds mentioned whose quills were used in the Middle Ages seem to be swan, pheasant, duck, eagle, crow and even pelicans. (I have seen an enormous pen, made by a friend from a condor quill.) Paper was not used extensively for books in Europe until the fourteenth century, although it had been used in China since about 105 A.D.

Scribes were not necessarily well educated or even able to read the Latin texts which they copied; but their writing skills, due to much practice, were highly developed. In the same way that the Sumerian pictograms became new cuneiform shapes, through being copied and slightly changed in the process, so did many of the Roman letters become altered by succeeding generations of scribes. (See chart overleaf.)

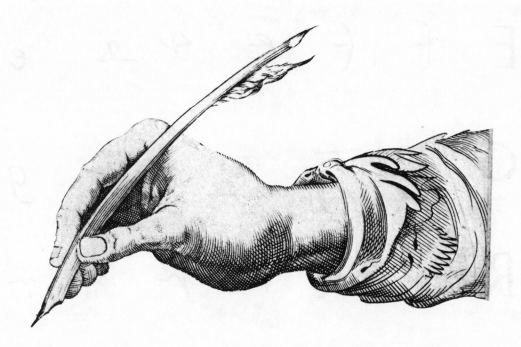

*Chart of how some Roman Capitals
changed their shapes from being copied by hand
down the centuries*

A A Λ Λ Λ d a a a

B B B b b b b

D D D O a b b d

E E F e θ e e

G G G 5 g g g

R R R Λ r r

*The Labour of Writing by a Medieval Scribe*

The labour of the writer is the refreshment of the reader. The one depletes the body, the other advances the mind. Whoever you are, therefore, do not scorn but be mindful of the work of one labouring to bring you profit . . . If you do not know how to write you will consider it no hardship but if you want a detailed account of it, let me tell you the work is heavy; it makes the eyes misty, bows the back, crushes the ribs and belly, brings pain to the kidneys and makes the body ache all over. Therefore, O reader, turn the leaves gently and keep your fingers away from the letters, for as the hailstorm ruins the harvest of the land so does the unserviceable reader destroy the book and its writing. As the sailor finds welcome in the final harbour, so does the scribe the final line. Deo gratias semper.

The scribes had a hard and often boring task. Imagine copying out the whole Bible several times! It is no wonder that many of them wrote personal notes in the margins and enjoyed decorating the pages with little drawings. In the tenth century an unknown scribe wrote at the side of a manuscript page:

Scribere qui nescit, nullam putat esse laboram.
He who knows not how to write thinks it no labour.

And another scribe wrote:

> Vinum scriptori reddatur de meliori.
> Let the best wine be given to the writer.

The task of the scribe in those days included preparing his own skins for the vellum, making his own inks from various recipes, and cutting and mending his quills.

Qui scribere nescit nullam putat esse laboram. Tres digit scribant, duo oculi vident. Una lingua loquitur. Totum corpus laborat, et omnis labor finem habet. Et praemium ejus non habet finem.

(Ignorant people think the scribe's profession an easy one. Three fingers are engaged in writing, the two eyes in looking: your tongue pronounces the words and the whole body toils. But all labour comes to an end, though its reward shall have no end. Gospel M.S. 8th century.)

A medieval scribe employed by the Lord Chancellor's office once wrote that he was 'closeted in my wardrobe forty days without surcease' in order to complete his work.

In the eighth century Alcuin of York and later of Tours in France, wrote in his book 'On Orthography':

It is a noble task to transcribe holy books, nor shall that scribe fail to have the reward that will be waiting for him in his work. The writing of books is superior to the cultivating of vines, for the man who tends a vine is taking care of his own belly, whereas he who writes a book is serving his own soul.

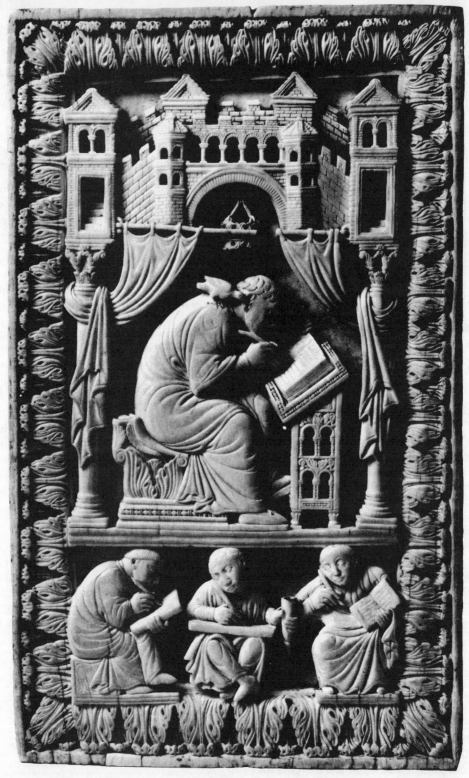

*Saint Gregory with Three Scribes. Carving from the Kunsthistorisches Museum, Vienna.*

## The Chancery Cursive or 'Italian' Hand

Italic or Italian handwriting was originally called in Latin, Cancelleresca Corsiva – the Chancery Cursive. It is generally believed that Pope Eugenius IV decreed that all Papal Briefs should be more legibly written in this style some time early in the sixteenth century.

Sixty or seventy years earlier a scholar from Florence, Niccolo de Niccoli, had developed a fast joined hand based upon the Carolingian minuscules. This was the style which Pope Eugenius' chief scribes took as their model. In 1522 one of them, called Ludovico degli Arrighi (sometimes known as Vicentino), published *La Operina* which is now known as 'The First Writing Book'. Reproduced by hand-cut wood blocks, it was one of the main sources of teaching the Cancelleresca Corsiva throughout Christendom:

Dal
primo adunq
Tratto piano et gros-
so cioe' - - - che' alla riuersa
& tornando per il medesmo se' incom-
mincia,
principiarai tutte' le'infrascritte' littere'
-abcdfghklogssx
xyz
Lo resto poi delo Alphabeto se'principia
dalo
secundo Tratto acuto
et sottile' con il taglio dela penna asce-
dendo et poi
allo ingue
Ritornando in questo modo designato
·iee'imnprtuÿ·

Diuisiones 4º Aprilis die Mercurij.

1. Omnis honestas manat e quatuor partibus quarū una sit cognitionis altera communitatis tertia est magnanimitatis et elationis animi quarta moderationis.

2. Delicta alia sunt magna quae facile apparent alia sunt parua quæ plerunq̅ sunt abdita.

3. Duplex est uirtus una quæ posita est in actione altera uero consistit in cogitatione.

4. Alij student quo modo possint eloqui alij copiose prudenterq̅, alij cogitare optime scire eloquentia.

5. Rogamus et inquirimus non solū quid quisque se loquatur, sed etiam quid quisq̅ sentiat et qua de causa ita quis sentiat.

## DEFINITIONES.

1. Prudentia est scientia rerum expetendarū et fugiendarū.
2. Sapientia est scientia rerum diuinarū et humanarum.
3. Iustitia est societas ac communitas uniuersi generis humani.
4. Eloquentia eos complectitur quibuscū uiuimus amore.
5. Cogitatio uertitur in se ipsa.
6. Temperantia est ommium rerū moderatio

Finis. Recitationis primi libri·

Edward VI's Latin book as a schoolboy.

Until printing began in Europe in the fifteenth century, professional clerks were employed to write letters and documents. This is still done in India and some other Eastern countries today. Very few people could read, other than the clergy and monks. In fact, the word 'clericus' came to mean someone who could write, and we still refer to priests as 'clerics'. When we bear in mind that heiroglyphic means 'the secret writing of the priests' and remember that 'runic' means mysterious, it becomes clear that universal literacy is a relatively recent demand.

It is generally considered that the Italian influence upon English handwriting was brought about by the introduction of the italic hand to the Court of Henry VII. His Latin Secretary was Petrus Carmelianus from Brescia. By the middle sixteenth century Sir John Cheke at Cambridge University was the leader of an influential group of scholars all writing an italic hand. One who certainly came under his influence was Ascham.

Roger Ascham, who was tutor both to the young Edward VI and to Elizabeth I, was born in Yorkshire in 1515. He was educated at St. John's College, Cambridge and eventually made a Fellow and University Orator. It was his task to write the university's letters to the Court and to the king. His penmanship was famous. It was said of him that 'He wrote with such diligence and such elegance that nothing could be more finely written'. Ascham himself was pleased with the italic hand which he taught to his royal pupils. He wrote, 'I was sent for many times to teach the king (Edward VI) to write and brought him before he was eleven years old to write as fair a hand, though I say it, as any child in England.'

In England, by the mid fifteenth century, merchants and middle-class traders, doctors and lawyers were becoming writers. Families began to write informal letters to each other, and it was considered important for well-born youngsters to be able to write a fluent hand.

In the sixteenth century printing and engraving became firmly established crafts.

The ability to reproduce books and newssheets easily and to send them from one place to another quickly, brought about a new demand for education. More and more schools were founded, especially the small, local grammar schools. Many churches started village and parish schools.

Copy books began to be engraved and printed. The earliest writing books published in England were probably *A Booke Containing Divers Sortes of Hands* by John Baildon and John de Beauchesne in 1570 and *A Newe Booke of Copies*, 1574, published by Thomas Vautroullier. Some of the lines in the latter are in the form of hints to children:

Dish, Dash, long tayle flye false writing eschewe.

and

That none but best handes may always best please:
To writing belonges good things two or three:

Another famous writing master was Peter Bales, born in 1547 and educated at Oxford. He wrote a copybook in 1590 called *The Writing Schoolemaster* some lines from which are given below. He was famous for his microscopic writing and was known to have copied out a complete Bible so small that it could fit into a walnut shell.

How to hold a pen

Betweene your thumb and your two fingers place
Your pen to write with comlines and grace.
Your thumb first aloft, as highest bestowe,
Your forefinger next, your middle belowe.
Hold softly your pen, lean lightlie thereon,
Write softlie therewith, and pause thereupon;
For swiftness will come of itself anon.
Ill tricks are soon caught, but not so soone gon.

from *The Writing Schoolemaster* by Peter Bales
1590

The best known early copybook is probably *The Pen's Excellence or The Secretary's Delight* by Martin Billingsley published in 1616. Billingsley was writing master to Charles I when he was the Prince of Wales.

A famous competition between the writing masters Daniel Johnson and Peter Bales took place on Michaelmas Day 1595. The trophy was a Golden Pen worth twenty pounds, which was a very rich prize in those days. Writing masters at that time were expected to be able to write Hebrew, Syrian, Greek, Saxon, Gothic and so on. Many writers claimed to teach at least a hundred different styles.

Bales and Johnson's competition stayed level for some hours, each able to match the other with writing styles. Finally Peter Bales produced his winner, 'Secretary and Roman hand four ways varied' and won the duel. Johnson claimed that Bales had cheated and that he had 'wheedled the precious golden pen out of the judges on the pretext of showing it to his sick wife. But the decision stood. Bales later pawned the golden pen.

*A copper plate engraver at work*

## The Rise of Copperplate

By the early eighteenth century England began to flourish as an international trading nation. And rather like the Phoenicians of old, the necessity for speedy legible writing made the quarrels about so many different styles seem rather outdated.

A neat, practical hand developed based upon the Italic model for bookkeeping and commercial use. Skilled penmen indulged in all sorts of loops and flourishes to demonstrate their art, and the copper engravers, when reproducing the copy books, added decorations too. From 1680 to 1740 almost every year saw the publication of another copy book. In 1740 George Bickham, the engraver, published 'The Universal Penman' which is a masterpiece, 212 pages of examples in the copperplate style.

The term 'copperplate' arises from the use of a plate of copper upon which the engraver incised his design (a copy of the writing master's page made back to front) for printing. The engraving was done with a pointed steel tool known as a burin. The deep cuts made the thick strokes, and the shallow cuts made the thin ones.

# The Invention of the Steel Pen

In a manuscript dated 1748 in the library of Aix-la-Chapelle a French writer named Johann Janssen wrote, 'It is perhaps not an accident that God should have inspired me at the present time with the idea of making steel pens, for all the envoys here assembled have bought the first that have been made, therewith as may be hoped to sign a treaty of peace, which with God's blessing shall be as permanent as the hard steel with which it is written. Of these pens as I have invented them, no man hath before seen or heard; if kept clean and free from rust and ink, they will continue fit for use for many years.'

In the 1780s in Paris the 'plume de fer' was severely frowned upon in schools and a boy found in possession of such an object was reprimanded and the pen banished. In England such pens were only just tolerated, and the way to favouritism was to write with a quill and to be able to mend it yourself!

In England in 1830 James Perry made the first commercially marketable steel slit pen with a hole at the slit base.

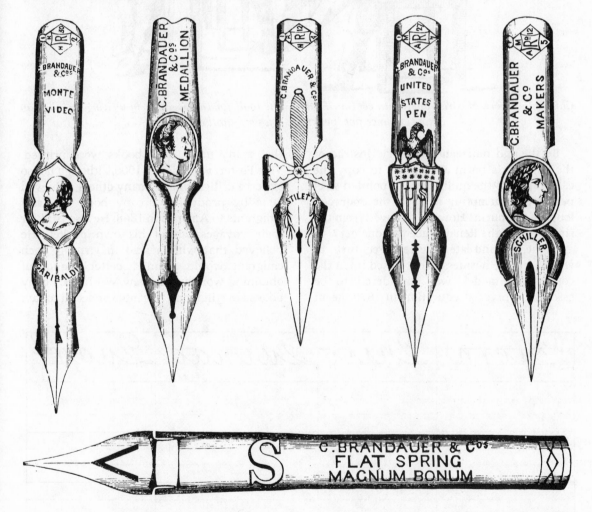

*Steel pen nibs from an 1862 catalogue reflect the Victorian's love of ornate and unusual decoration.*

*Children at work in early nineteenth century France. The tools for the beginner in writing included an inkpot, pounce pot, penknife, scissors, quill and slate.*

By the mid nineteenth century, instead of the engraver's burin attempting to copy the calligraphy of the quill, users of pointed steel pens were attempting to copy the engraved loops of the burin! How far removed from the simplicity of the Renaissance can one get?

In the mid and late nineteenth century, to write a legible business hand, based upon the copperplate model, was considered to be essential. Universal education in 1870 meant that many more copy books were printed. Vere Foster, who died in 1900, although not so expert a calligrapher as many others, achieved fame by producing a copy book for Irish emigrants to America in 1868. He also paid for their voyages out of his own pocket. He believed that with a skill in writing, each emigrant would stand a better chance of obtaining work in the New World. His copy books are still being reprinted and sold today.

*Quorn  Quito  Quinag  Quarf*

*From Vere Foster's copybook 3.*

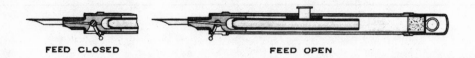

FEED CLOSED          FEED OPEN

## "PENOGRAPHIC" FOUNTAIN PEN, ca. 1819.

"Reservoir pens" were known in the 17th. century, Samuel Pepys having recorded that he had one in 1663. The first two British patents were taken out in 1809 and the example exhibited is of the type which formed the subject of the third patent, by John Scheffer ten years later. It includes features which are more nearly in keeping with later practice.

The ink feed to the nib is controlled by a cock which must be closed before the cap can be replaced on the pen. Accidental leakage is thus prevented. The flow of ink to the nib was started, and had to be periodically refreshed by pressure on a lever in the side of the pen. The lever pressed upon a quill tube covered with layers of sheep gut, and as a cork made the ink reservoir air-tight this pressure forced ink through the aperture to the nib. The sheep gut was simply a device for making a suitable bond between the flexible quill reservoir and the solid metal of the pen structure. When the gut was swollen by contact with the ink this bond became very firm.

For further particulars see Patent No. 4389/1819.

INV. 1938-125.

Originally called the Ideal Safety Pen, the pen which contained its own ink was invented by Lewison Waterman, an American, in 1884. It is said that Waterman, who was an insurance salesman at that time, gave an important client a quill pen and a bottle of ink to sign a document. The pen splattered ink and ruined the contract. Waterman rushed away to fetch a spare copy, but in the meantime a rival insurance man got the client to sign another contract.

This incident made Waterman furious and he went on to design a pen which would contain its own ink.

# Interesting Facts About Writing

This section contains a treasure trove of bits of information which children will find interesting. They are arranged very roughly in chronological order. Older children may like to refer to this section when making a topic book on the history of the alphabet or handwriting. Teachers may find that one or two of the incidents may liven up a handwriting lesson for them.

# Starting Points for Project Work

Three things bear mighty sway with men,
The sword, the sceptre and the pen;
Who can the least of these command,
In the first rank of fame will stand.

Geo Bickham, *The Universal Penman*, 1743

*A Riddle* from Anglo-Saxon Poems in the Exeter Book, probably 8th century.

I am the scalp of myself, skinned by my foeman:
robbed of my strength, he seeped and soaked me,
dipped me in water, whipped me out again,
set me in the sun. I soon lost there
the airs I had had.
     The hard edge
of a keen-ground knife cuts me now,
fingers fold me, and a fowl's pride
drives its treasure trail across me,
bounds again over the brown rim,
sucks the wood-dye steps on me again,
makes his black marks.
     A man then hides me
between stout shield-boards stretched with hide,
fits me with gold. There glows on me
the jewelsmith's handiwork held with wires.
Let these royal enrichments and this red dye
and splendid settings spread the glory
of the Protector of peoples – and plague the fool.
If the sons of men will make use of me
they shall . . .

(from *The Earliest English Poems* translated by
 Michael Alexander published by Penguin Books)

## The Persistent Thorn

The early northern European runic writing contained the sign þ known as 'thorn'. Its phonic value was the sound th. In the 15th century, when documents came to be written in English, the þ sign gradually became contracted to a ɣ shape so that an abbreviated form of 'the' was written as ɣᵉ . In this form, remember that it is not a capital Y, and the word therefore should still be pronounced as 'The'. We still see it today as 'Ye Olde Tea Shoppe'.

## Which are vowels and which are consonants?

In Latin, the letters I and J were interchangeable and in the capital alphabet only I existed. U and V were also counted as the same letter and W, although called 'double U' in England, arose as a 'double V' in Latin and is known as 'double vee' in most European languages.

The convention which suggests that i and u are vowels and j and v are consonants was not generally accepted in England until as late as the 17th century. Thus in earlier documents, words such as vpon and neuer for upon and never are quite common.

## It's All Greek to Me!

Greek was virtually unknown to the Medieval Scribes who wrote in Latin only. A standard phrase used by monks (who nevertheless copied many ancient Greek texts and thus preserved them for us) was
'Graeca sunt, non legitur.'
meaning
'These words are Greek so they cannot be read'!

## The Care of Books

*Burning*. It is said that the Crusaders at the conquest of Constantinople in 1204 burned about 120,000 volumes.

*Stabbing*. The books of Virgil were considered to be prophetic and to foretell the future. In ancient times people would stick a needle into a book, then open the page where the needle had reached. They would then read the text. As a result many of the old manuscripts are said to look more like sieves!

## How the i became dotted

The dot on the small letter i and j was a small mark placed by some scribes from about 1230

121

A.D. onwards in order to signify the letter i when it was concealed among similar letters. e.g.

ínímíca quíeta

During the 15th century, scribes more often avoided putting a dot on the i by using the letter y instead. e.g.

myne lyßyngo

## The Ampersand

The best known signs are usually a contracted version of the Latin 'et' meaning 'and'. Such abbreviations have been used for thousands of years. The word 'ampersand' is a contraction of 'and per se and', i.e. '& by itself makes and.'

## The confusing minims

Scribes took little care, in their formal book hands, to distinguish between the minims u, v, n, m and r; and in the strictly mechanical Gothic it is very difficult to read many Latin words e.g.

mınımum

The well-known words of the Te Deum ending '. . . make us to be numbered (numerare) with thy saints' originally read in the Latin '. . . make us to be rewarded (munerare) with thy saints'. It was probably misread many years ago due to the illegibility of the Gothic book hand.

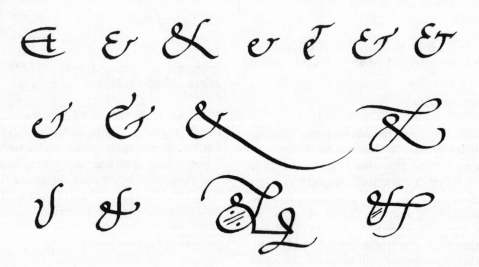

122

*The Origin of the Question Mark*

Q stands for Question. It also stands for Quaere, the Latin word for question. In early manuscripts the word quaere was often written after a sentence to indicate that it was a question. Later this was abbreviated to Q.

The original semitic form of this letter was φ which originated from a pictogram meaning 'monkey'. Thus the real history of our question mark is probably a monkey's tail! Nowadays the query sign also has a period or full stop beneath it in order to indicate the end of a question or sentence, e.g. Will you remember?

*A Famous Pen-Twister of the 14th Century*

mimi numimum niuium
minimi munium nimium
umi muminimum imminui
uiui minimum uolunt

*'One jot or tittle'*

This is a joke letter supposed to have been sent to the Roman Senate by short actors who did not wish to give up distributing wine from vineyards near the city walls. Literally translated it reads:

The very short mimes of the snow-gods do not at all wish that during their lifetime the very great burden of (distributing) the wine of the walls be lightened.

It is of course just a scribe's piece of fun with the 'Gothic' minims used at the time. You can very clearly see the value of the iota over the letter 'i'.

The jot or iota (nowadays it has become known as the dot) was the smallest kind of mark used by scribes in early times. It was used to represent the beads on an abacus until the 15th century when Arabic numerals became more widely used. The iota therefore signified the smallest unit in a calculation. Later a dot was put over the small letter i. In the early Hebrew alphabet, the jot was the smallest sign, hence our present word 'jottings' for little notes, and a 'jotter' for writing them in!

The tittle was a short line, sometimes straight and sometimes wavy, put over a letter or a line of letters signifying a shortened form

in medieval times
e.g.

 for man

 for in.

*ffoulkes with two small fs!*

Up until the 13th century, the manuscripts written in Gothic hands decorated the capital letters and exaggerated some features until the letter was almost unrecognisable. The capital F, however, was usually written as a large minuscule
e.g.

A fashion for placing internal lines paralleling the main strokes had existed for some time and letters such as O, E, P and T were written as

So a vertical line was added to the capital F, giving various forms of the letter, looking like this

Eventually, later scrivenors (scribes) perceived this embellishment as a double f and the fanciful conceit of an aristocratic surname beginning with two small fs was born.

There is a charming story of a baby girl who was being christened in church a few years ago. When asked by the vicar what he should name the child, the godparent said she should be called 'Alfo'. Surprised, the vicar asked where the name came from, as he had never come across it before. The child's father stepped forward and pointed to a 17th century gravestone carved and set into the church floor. It read

*In Loving Memory of Thoˢ Reed & Mary Reed & Alſo their daughter*

---

The long s, which so resembles an f to modern eyes, has a respectable history. It is only a fanciful stretching of the letter s in a decorative manner and is found on the wax tablets of the early Roman cursive, and in the half uncials of the 8th century. By the close of the 13th century the long s was sometimes used in book hands, but in cursive writing began to develop a looped tail ſ , making it appear even more f-like to us. In those days, however, it was perfectly legible. Ludovico Arrighi, in his writing book published in Rome in 1522, teaches both the long ſ and the small s.

The letter survived well into the 18th century as an affectation, and can be found in Geo. Bickham's *Universal Penman*, published in 1743, in such words as

*Busineſs    Scripſit*

*Aſsistance    Deſire Loſt*

*Cheriſh'd    Perſons*

*A Chancy Life!*

Pierre Hamon who wrote an alphabet book published in Paris in 1567 was the royal writing master and secretary to King Charles IX of France. He was accused of forging the king's signature and hanged. All his books were ordered to be destroyed.

John Scottowe who published a manuscript copybook in 1592 was a schoolmaster in Norwich. In 1597 he was excommunicated for teaching without a licence.

It seems as if it was not always easy to be a writing master. One of the greater temptations for someone who could write perfectly in a hundred different styles, was forgery!

*A Ready Way for children to learn their A.B.C.*

Cause four large dice of bone or wood to be made, and upon every square one of the small letters of the cross row to be graven, but in some bigger shape, and the child using to play much with them, and being always told what letter chanceth, will soon gain his alphabet, as it were by the way of sport or pastime.

Sir Hugh Plat *Jewel House of Art and Nature* 1635

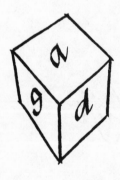 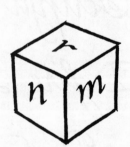 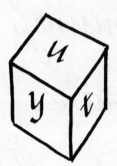 

From: *Teaching Reading in Early England* by Frank Davies, Lecturer in Education, University of Southampton, Pitman Publishing, London 1973.

Most people read most easily what they are most accustomed to, and since the ordinary conditions accustom them to bad writing, they will often consider that more legible than good writing.

Robert Bridges 1899

Much argument ebbs and flows between 'experts' upon the readability of different scripts and alphabets. The truth is that readability is extremely subjective, as are all forms of visual perception. There is as much influence from the background and experience of the person doing the reading as there is from the type of script. Indeed, no one script can be said to be obviously unreadable compared with another; so much depends upon the prejudices of the reader.

One may argue that

*Palimpsest* is more readable than *Palimpsest*

or vice versa!

---

In fact, with very little practice, an adult or a child can become familiar with almost any style from Anglo Saxon to the Secretary Hand.

Try reading the following. It is written in the Elizabethan Secretary Hand.

*Dear Sir,*

*I beseech you most sincerely to note most carefully what I have to say.*

Now look at it more carefully again and you will gradually realise, letter by letter, that you can read it without a transcript. The readability of the piece has not changed and yet it has become easier. It is the subjective abilities of you, the reader, which have changed through this little experience. It is amazing how, even when distorted by these mannered capitals, the essentially Roman alphabet is still legible to us. Now you should find the next two lines much easier to read than the first two:

*At Christmas time the Olde Clock Chymes rynge out to Wish us all goodwill.*

By a small amount of application it is quite possible for any able reader to pick up enough experience to read old manuscripts in English.

The readability of a well-produced print style and the readability of an individual person's handwriting are, of course, two quite different matters. A print style has usually been evolved, however fancifully, in order to communicate and has a designed consistency about it. Personal handwriting, unless well taught, can deteriorate under pressure of speed, tiredness, age or illness and become unreadable even to its writer. It is the *inconsistency* of bad or tired handwriting which makes for illegibility. In teaching handwriting, therefore, it is the consistency of shapes, slopes and heights which will make for good legibility. Character and style will develop independently.

*The Writing Master's class.*

*On a Pen*

In youth exalted high in air,
Or bathing in the waters fair,
Nature to form me took delight
And clad my body all in white.
My person tall, and slender waist,
On either side with fringes graced;
Till me that tyrant man espied,
And dragged me from my mother's side:
My skin he flayed, my hair he cropped:
At head and foot my body lopped:
And then, with heart more hard than stone,
He picked my marrow to the bone.
To vex me more, he took a freak
To slit my tongue and make me speak:
But, that which wonderful appears,
I speak to eyes, and not to ears.
He oft employs me in disguise,
And makes me tell a thousand lies.
All languages I can command,
Yet not a word I understand.
But while I thus my life relate,
I only hasten on my fate.
My tongue is black, my mouth is furred,
I hardly now can force a word.
I die unpitied and forgot,
And on some dunghill left to rot.

Jonathan Swift 1667–1745

*How to sit when Writing – from Cassell's
Popular Education 1853*

What can be more absurd than to see a boy or girl
sprawling on a table or desk with their arms
akimbo, and their noses upon the paper imitating
the motion of the pen? What more foolish or
disagreeable than to see every stroke of the pen
imitated by the mouth or the tongue, as if the
writer was approaching a state of idiocy?

Let every student of penmanship sit erect like a
lady or gentleman while writing and let him only
stoop his head with gentle inclination, as we said
before, sufficient to enable him to see clearly what
he is doing. . . .

*The smallest handwriting*

Larry R. Yates of McMinnville, Oregon, U.S.A.
has manually engraved the Lord's Prayer
within a square millimetre $1/645 \ in^2$ with a
pivot-arm device of his own invention. Frank
C. Watts of Felmingham, Norfolk de-
monstrated for photographers on 24 Jan. 1968,
his ability, without mechanical or optical aid,
to write the Lord's Prayer 34 times (9,452
letters) within the size of a definitive U.K.
postage stamp (viz.) 0.84 × 0.71 of an inch
*21.1 × 18.2 mm.*

*Guinness Book of Records*

*Learning to Write in the USSR*

In the USSR children do not start formal
schooling until the age of seven. But the Soviet
kindergarten begins at the age of two months
and goes on until the seventh year. Half way
through this seventh year, school preparation
begins. The official programme of instruction
states that in the second quarter of the
children's seventh year (that is when the
children are six and a half years old) they
should be 'introduced to the sounds and
letters МШрS (m, sh, r and s are the phonic
equivalents), they should be taught to pro-
nounce these sounds, to notice them in words
and syllables and to know how to print them.
The teacher explains what a page is, what a
line is, and how to sit properly and hold their
pencils and notebooks correctly. The children
trace lines and draw designs. The teacher gets
the children ready for writing with special
exercises and teaches them to draw the basic
elements of the various letters with a pencil. In
the third quarter of the year the children are
familiarised with the sounds and letters
ЛНрП (l, n, r, p are the phonetic equivalents). From cardboard letters the children put
together syllables and words, first using the
vowels "a", y, o and ы . Drills in writing the
basic elements of the letters continue.'

AaБaBaГaДaEaЖ

ЖиЗиИиКиКиКиЛиl

eMeHeOeПePeCeУe

TpФpXpЦpЧpЩpЭ

лЮлДлЯлЛлМлУл

DkEkGkIkJkLkNkS

sQsRsVsUsWsYsZs!

1q2q3t4t5r6r7f8i9

## Useful Contractions of Words

For the sake of speed, it has long been a tradition in informal writing such as in personal notes or letters to friends, to use abbreviations of common words.

In recent years this useful aid to economy seems almost to have disappeared. If taught in schools the practice may become common again. Here is a list of some of the widely accepted contractions in English. They are in alphabetical order. Full stops are not used for contractions for the obvious reason of speed!

& – and
&c – etcetera
abt – about
aftn – afternoon
altho – although
alw – always
anon – anonymous
bn – been
btwn – between
cd – could
cf – compare(d)
cm – centimetre(s)
ctee – committee
diff – difference, different
eg – for example
Eng – England, English
esp – especially
ex – out of
fr – from
gal – gallon
gm – gramme(s)
ie – that is
info – information
int – interest, interesting
lit – literally
math – mathematics
mech – mechanic(al)
med – medical, medicine
mod – modern
MS – manuscript
mtg – meeting
nb – note well

neg – negative
pp – pages
prob – probably
ref – reference
secy – secretary
shd – should
tech – technical
tho – though
v – very
vol – volume
w – with
wd – word, would
wh – which
yr – your
yrs – yours

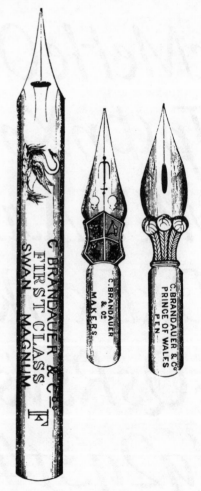

# Things To Do

Friar Pacificus speaks:

God forgive me – I seem to feel
A certain satisfaction steal
Into my heart and into my brain,
As if my talent had not lain
Wrapped in a napkin all in vain;
Yes, I might almost say to the Lord:
Here is a copy of Thy Word,
Written out with much toil and Pain.
Take it, O Lord, and let it be
As something I have done for thee.

From the *Golden Legend* by Longfellow

*Introduction*

When children have been learning to write well, teachers sometimes feel that they would like to give them some activities other than merely writing stories or exercises. The activities suggested here are just a few starting points for creative uses of the pen. They are particularly suited to the needs of older primary children who have acquired some calligraphic skill and who would like to go further in exercising and developing their powers of penmanship.

133

# 1. Cutting a quill pen

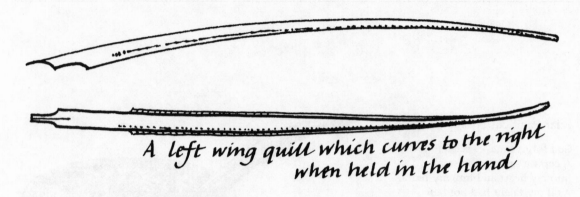

*A left wing quill which curves to the right when held in the hand*

The word *pen* comes from the Latin *penna* – a feather. Since at least 150 B.C. scribes and scrivenors have used the outer wing feathers of birds for pens. It is assumed that the quill came into common use when vellum took the place of papyrus as a writing surface around 190 B.C. The larger birds such as swan, goose and turkey have the biggest and strongest wing feathers, and it is usually the first five flight feathers which are used. Some artists used raven and crow wing feathers for fine drawing, but in general the larger the quill, the easier it is to cut and use.

In Britain, October and November are good months to obtain quills from the farms and factories plucking for Christmas. If you find a local supply and tell them why you want the quills, you will usually be overwhelmed with them as otherwise they are merely burned.

The professional scribe spent a good deal of time 'dutching' or 'clarifying' the feathers in preparation for pen making, and for full details consult the *Calligrapher's Handbook* published by Faber & Faber Limited, Queen Square, London.

Very satisfactory quill pens can be cut by the amateur or by children with a little practice. Primary school children can become absolutely fascinated by quill work.

Note that the scribe cuts off the barbs of the feather which get in the way when writing. Paintings and prints of important people signing documents with a full feather are presumably records of rather special events.

To prepare a quill you will need a very sharp blade indeed. A surgical scalpel or dissecting knife is best. Otherwise a safety razor blade or a brand new craft knife blade may do. The old 'pen-knives' were of a special design and were kept absolutely razor sharp.

Scrape away rough outer skin from the barrel of the quill, and remove the feather barbs. (These can be used for arrow flights for the archery fans!) Balance the quill in the writing hand for comfort to see upon which side you want to cut the nib. Then, as if sharpening a pencil, make a good strong cut from the writing end.

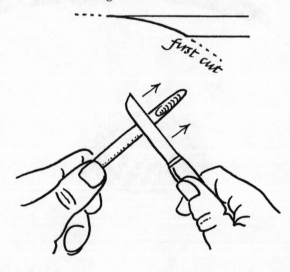

*first cut*

Next, with the knife point or tweezers, pull the dry membranes out from inside the quill. This is easier if the quill has been gently heated and dried on a radiator for a few hours. Now cut the end of the nib off square, by a downward press of the knife onto a plastic or formica surface

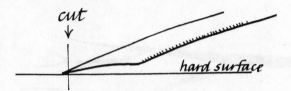

and make the ink flow slit about 5 mm long.

Now make your next cuts on each side of the nib by pulling the knife towards you in a paring movement.

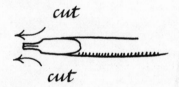

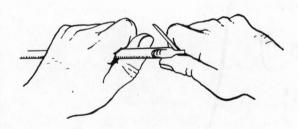

By this means you can decide how broad the writing point is to be. For normal writing purposes about 1 mm is suitable. Finally you may need to re-cut across the end of the nib with a clean downward chop onto the hard

surface. In close-up the cut quill should end up looking like this

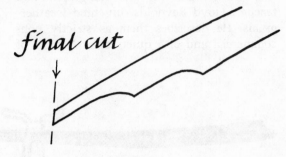

Without a reservoir the ink will run out after one or two words. Experiment with a piece of cotton wool pushed up the barrel or a strip of tin foil cut and bent as shown.

Tin foil should be in contact with the ink slit.

*Nylon Tubing Quills*

Nylon tubing or polypropylene tube, about 8 mm in diameter, can be used to cut a very pleasant 'quill' pen. It has a smooth touch and should be cut and split exactly as described for the goose quill. Ready-cut plastic quills can be obtained from
Braun Writing Instruments,
15 Georgia Drive,
Syosset,
New York, 11791 USA. Approx. $3 inc. p & p.

## 2. Weathergrams

The distinguished American calligrapher and teacher, Lloyd Reynolds, invented weathergrams. He describes them as strictly non-commercial and of a quiet style. A piece of tough brown paper of the grocery bag variety is cut, about ten inches by two and a half inches (25 cm by 5 cm), and a very short poem of about ten words or less is written on the paper.

An inch
of puddle
reflects
miles of
sky

Reynolds used Higgins waterproof ink and an informal italic style of writing. The weathergram may be hung in a bush or tree to 'weather' and to amuse passers by. It may be given to a friend as a little thank you.

Weathergrams are charming, and although Americans might consider them an oriental idea, Europeans would classify them as representing that very engaging aspect of gentle Americans.

Some of Lloyd Reynolds' examples of weathergram poems are quoted, but readers are urged to make up their own. They are very similar to the Japanese three-line senryu.

*At the cliff's edge
the only
direction
is down*
*

*mountain   mountain
waterfall
stream*
*

*After watching
seagulls
feeling my weight
in my shoes
again*
*

*Maple leaves
come spinning down
Air Mail
Special Delivery
Reply Urgent*
*

## 3. Flourishes

For hundreds of years, those who practised writing with a pen have enjoyed making elaborate flourishes and twirls. Scribes and writing masters used these decorations to fill empty corners on pages, and to liven up capital letters, especially the first or initial letter on a page. The more serious-minded writing masters in the 17th century were rather critical of some of the rather showy 'knots' and 'flourishes'. Edward Cocker (1631–1676) was extremely skilled at drawing knots and claimed that those who did not like such decorations were only jealous because they could not draw them themselves. He wrote:

> Some sordid sotts
> Cry down rare knotts
> But art shall shine
> And envies pine
> And still my pen shall flourish.

Try a few of these!

138

## 4. Shaped Writing

It is a very old tradition to use blocks of writing to form a picture or a pattern. Chinese writing has always been admired for its visual pattern as well as its meaning. The Burmese, Malayans, Indians, Moroccans, Arabs and other cultures have all used shaped writing. In modern times the Concrete Poetry movement has re-awakened an interest in this ancient art.

Here are a few ideas to give you something to think about. A good resource book for finding historical examples is 'The Word as Image' by Berjouhi Bowler, published by Studio Vista, London. Some more ideas are given in 'Fun With Pens' by Christopher Jarman, published by A. & C. Black Limited.

leaf leaf leaf
tree tree tree tree tree
leaf tree tree tree leaves
leaves bird's leaf leaves tree
tree nest leaves tree tree
leaf leaves tree tree tree
leaf tree leaf branch leaf
leaf branch branch
branch branch
trunk trunk
trunk
trunk
roots roots roots
roots roots roots roots roots roots
roots roots roots roots roots
roots roots roots
roots roots

The clear wide blue sky above
cloud & cloud
cloud
The long distant horizon at the eye's limit
and the long
road winding
its way home

egg

FALLING

hopping

hanged drawn & quartered

## 5. Acronyms and Acrostics

Here are some acronyms to copy for practice.
An acronym is a word formed from the initial
letters of other words as you will see.

Light
Amplification by
Simulated
Emission of
Radiation

North
Atlantic
Treaty
Organisation

R }
A } radio
Detecting
And
Ranging

Royal
Academy of
Dramatic
Art

Brackets
Of (x)
Division
Multiplication
Addition
Subtraction

BODMAS *is the order for working out all maths calculations.*

An acrostic is sometimes a poem, sometimes just a group of letters, in which the first or last letters of each line, taken in order, spell a word or saying.

This famous Roman acrostic was found by archaeologists on the wall of a house excavated in Cirencester in Gloucestershire. It is thought to date from about 79 A.D. and is probably a secret sign indicating the presence of a Christian family.

```
R O T A S
O P E R A
T E N E T
A R E P O
S A T O R
```

```
      P
      A
      T
      E
      R
P A T E R N O S T E R
      O
      S
      T
      E
      R
```

As well as being an acrostic, the square contains four words that make other words backwards, and a palindrome – TENET.

✳

The letters also make the anagram of PATERNOSTER which means Our Father.

✳

When rearranged as follows,
```
S A T O R
A R E P O
T E N E T
```
It is thought to read in Latin, "Sat orare poten" meaning "Are you able to pray enough?"

141

## 6. Decorated Borders

Many children like to decorate the borders of a page of writing. This is a fine old practice and it is a pity to spoil a beautifully written page of work with a hurried scribble of thick crayon, or a careless scrawl of ink. Why not learn some of the traditional designs and then adapt them for modern use?

The handwriting patterns given earlier in this book make good borders, while providing excellent practice too. Combinations of letters, some upside down, can always be used. I have

seen sentences or repeated words, used to put round a border. Do not overlook the decorative effect of coloured inks too.

Beware of making border patterns too big. The most effective unit size is about the same, or even smaller than the writing on the page Good books suggesting border patterns and page layouts are 'Make Your Own Booklet' by John le F. Dumpleton, published by A. & C. Black Limited and 'Cursive Handwriting' by Philip Burgoyne, published by Dryad Press.

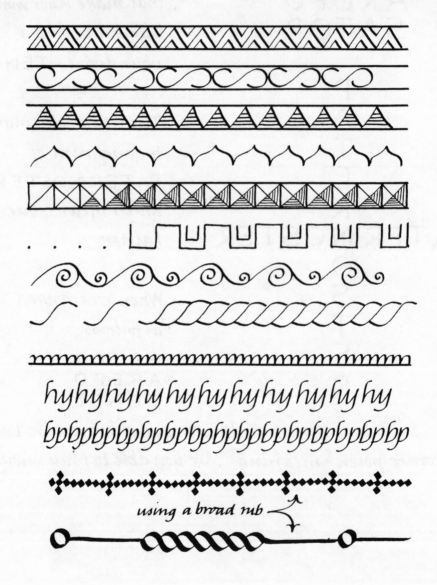

142

## 7. Writing in curves

The layout of a page of writing can be made more interesting if the writing is occasionally laid out in curved lines. Or perhaps the border could be written in an oval or some other shape. The easiest way to do this is first to decide on the curve you want, or upon the kind of wavy lines. Then draw your shape on a piece of thin card. Cut along the line and you have a template. Use this curved template like a ruler and with a light pencil draw your guidelines along the card edge.

143

## 8. How to Write in a Spiral

Some people delight in writing in spirals but I daresay very few recipients of these circumbendibi enjoy reading them! Nevertheless, in order for you to annoy your friends, here is a simple method. The trick is to draw a faint pencil spiral line first, write your note, and then rub out the guideline. The easiest way to draw the spiral is freehand. You just start in the middle of the page and spiral outwards, keeping the lines approximately 1 cm apart.

If you wish to be more mathematical then use a pair of compasses and draw five concentric *semicircles* as shown in the diagram. The first is 1 cm radius, the second 2 cm and so on. Next, move the compass point 0.5 cm (half a space) to the right and with a radius of 1.5 cm begin the spiral. Keeping this second centre, continue to complete the other set of concentric semicircles. The resulting shape is not a true spiral but it is quite suitable for a writing guide.

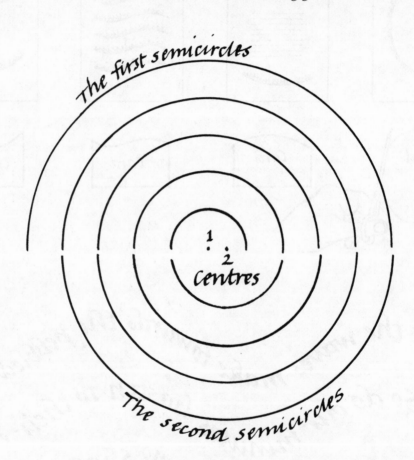

144

# TURKEYS by JOHN CLARE

The turkeys wade the close to catch the bees in the old border full of maple tres, and often lay and breed and come and bring a brood of chelping chickens home. The turkey gobbles loud and drops his rug and sprunts his tail and then lets drag his wing on ground and bounces up and flies at passer-by and drives the boys from play; they throw their sticks & kick and run away. He gobbles loud and makes a buzzing noise, nauntles the old snaps the boys and grins nor ventures nigh.

## 9. Decorated Capital Letters

Scribes have decorated the initial letters on pages of writing for more than a thousand years. The ways in which they chose to do this and the drawing styles they have used vary enormously. Certain styles were developed in some particular monasteries; and during different centuries new ways of decorating letters emerged. *Illuminated* letters are really letters made luminous or shiny by the use of

very thin sheets of gold known as gold leaf.

Some examples of traditional decoration are shown here. For more examples look in books on calligraphy, or better still try to see some original manuscripts. The Bodleian Library sells beautiful colour slides and small booklets of reproductions at very inexpensive rates. For full details write to The Keeper of Western Manuscripts, Bodleian Library, Oxford England.

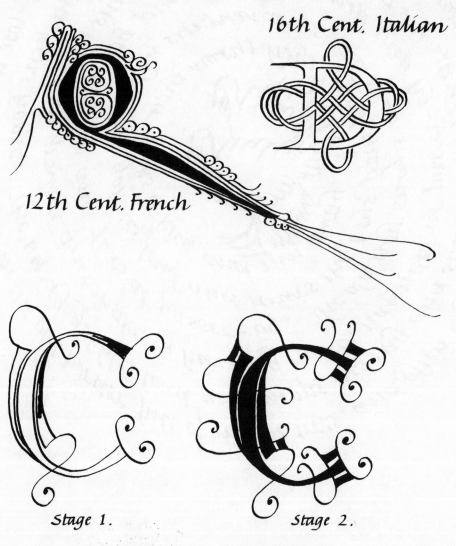

16th Cent. Italian

12th Cent. French

Stage 1.

Stage 2.

16th Cent. German

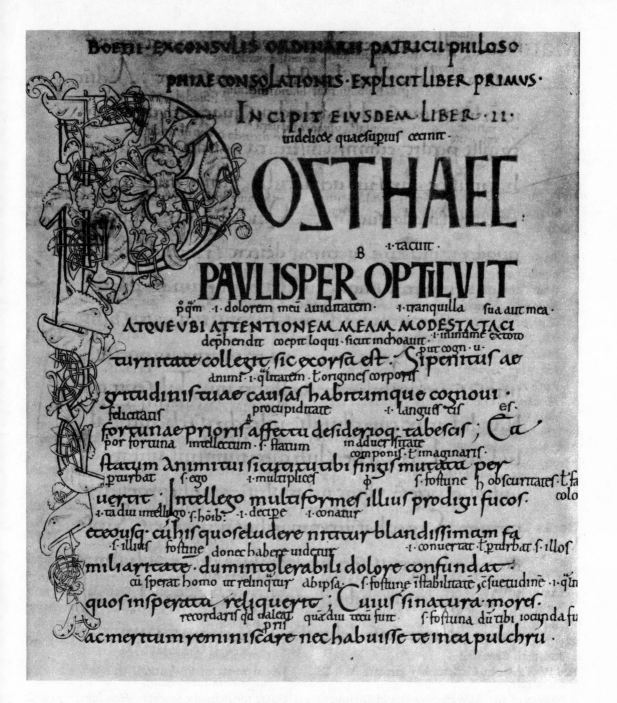

*The initial P from an Anglo Saxon illuminated manuscript in the Bodleian Library, Oxford.*

# Materials and Books

## Recommended copybooks and cards to supplement the copypages in this book

1. *Basic Modern Hand* and *wall chart* – handwriting cards by Christopher Jarman from Osmiroid Educational, Gosport.
2. *Beacon Writing Books* by Fairbank & Stone. Ginn & Co. Ltd.
3. *The Dryad Writing Cards* by Alfred Fairbank. Dryad Press.
4. *Everyday Writing Books* 1 & 2 only, by Ruth Fagg. University of London Press.
5. *Firsthand Writing* by Tom Barnard. Platignum Pen Co., Herts.
6. *The Nelson Handwriting Scheme* by Inglis & Gibson. Thos. Nelson & Sons Ltd.
7. *The Irene Wellington Copybook*. Pentalic Corp., N.Y.

## Books for Classroom Projects on Writing

*The Calligrapher's Handbook* Ed. by C. M. Lamb. Faber & Faber Ltd. containing comprehensive bibliography on handwriting and allied subjects.

*The Development of Handwriting*. Jackdaw. Jonathan Cape Ltd.

*Fun With Pens* by Christopher Jarman. A. & C. Black Ltd.

*A History of the Alphabet* by David Diringer. Unwin Bros. Ltd.

*Make Your Own Booklet* by John Dumpleton. A. & C. Black Ltd.

*The Story of Handwriting* by A. Fairbank. Faber & Faber Ltd.

*The Universal Penman* by Geo. Bickham. Dover Press Inc.

*The Young Calligrapher* by William Cartner. Kaye & Ward Ltd.

*Twenty Six Letters* by Oscar Ogg. Harrap & Co. Ltd.

## Materials and Books for Australia

*Modern Cursive Writing*: Linehan & Shrimpton

*Copy Books*: *Queensland*: Dominie.

*Styrene Writing Sheets*: Learning Research Pty Ltd.

*Effective Pre-Writing*: Nick Bricknell. Martin Educational.

*The Australian Lettering Book*: Angus and Robertson.

*Teacher References*

*What Did I Write?*: Marie Clay. Heinemann Educational.

Education Department of Victoria: *Course of Study for Primary Schools, Handwriting, 1964*.

Education Department of Victoria: *Language Curriculum Statement 1975*.

Department of Education, Queensland: *Language Arts Curriculum*.

*Guide for Primary Schools – Handwriting 1972*.

New South Wales Department of Education: *Curriculum for Primary Schools, Spelling and Handwriting*.

*Handwriting*: Moorabbin Inspectorate, Victoria 1978.

## Addresses for Equipment and Aids (in England)

*Vellum and Parchment*

Price list and samples available from
H. Band and Co.,
Brent way,
High Street,
Brentford, Middx.,
England.

*Calligraphy materials*

Pens, inks, handmade papers, quills, gold leaf etc.
Falkiner Fine Papers Limited,
4, Mart Street,
London WC2E 8DE     Tel. 01 240 2339

*Fountain Pens, Lettering sets, advisory service etc. and Wallcharts, Leaflets, Loan Exhibition of children's handwriting*

Osmiroid Educational,
Fareham Road,
Gosport,
Hants.

Platignum Pens,
Schools Division,
Six Hills Way,
Stevenage,
Herts.

*Film Strips of Early Manuscripts*

The Photographic Dept.,
Bodleian Library,
Oxford.

*Booksellers Specialising in Calligraphy*

Write for free catalogue to

Drummond, Bookseller,
30, Hart Grove,
Ealing,
London W5 3NB

Elkin Matthews,
Takeley,
Bishops Stortford,
Herts.

## American Suppliers of pens and books

The Pentalic Corporation,
132 W 22nd St.,
New York, 10011,
USA.

Museum Books Inc.,
48, East 43rd St.,
New York 10017,
USA

Hunt Manufacturing Co.
1405 Locust Street,
Philadelphia,
PA 19102,
USA

# Bibliography

Allport, G. W., *Pattern & Growth in Personality*. Holt, Rinehart & Winston. New York 1961.

Avi-Yonah, Michael, *Ancient Scrolls*. Cassell & Co. Ltd. London 1973.

Bowler, B. *The Word as Image*. Studio Vista. 1970.

Chauncey, H., *Soviet Pre-School Education* Vol. I. Holt, Rinehart & Winston. New York 1969.

Child, H., *Calligraphy Today*. Studio Vista. 1976.

Davies, F., *Teaching Reading in Early England*. Pitman & Sons Ltd. London 1973.

Diringer, D., *The Alphabet*. 2 vols. Hutchinson & Co. (Publishers) Ltd. London 1968.

Gray, N., 'Laying Down the Letter', *Times Educational Supplement* 19th August, 1977.

Grieve, H. E. P., *Examples of English Handwriting 1150–1750*. Essex Record Office. 1974.

Hector, L. C., *The Handwriting of English Documents*. Arnold (Edward) (Publishers) Ltd. 1966.

Johnston, E., *Formal Penmanship*. Lund Humphries (Percy) & Co. Ltd. 1971.

Whalley, J. I., *English Handwriting 1540–1853*. Victoria & Albert Museum H.M.S.O. 1969.

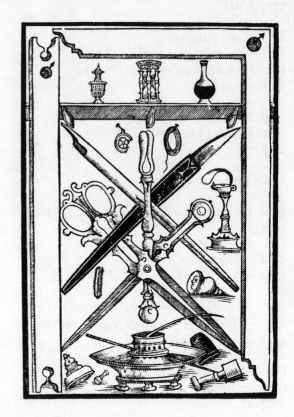